your Daddy, you know
your daddy said?
Why
Six
here
with a
she
gun
hand

ART WORKS

AUTOBIOGRAPHY

BARBARA STEINER AND JUN YANG

With 230 illustrations, 200 in colour

Thames & Hudson

With thanks to Ilina Koralova for the texts on Oliver Hangl,
Oliver Musovik, RASSIM® and Tracey Rose, and to Julia
Schäfer for the texts on Antje Schiffers and Moira Zoitl.

First published in the United Kingdom by
Thames & Hudson Ltd
181A High Holborn
London WC1V 7QX

www.thamesandhudson.com

British Library Cataloguing-in-Publication Data
A catalogue record for this book is available from the
British Library

ISBN 0-500-93005-8

Art direction and design by
Martin Andersen / Andersen M Studio

Printed and bound in China by C & C Offset Printing Co Ltd

CONTENTS

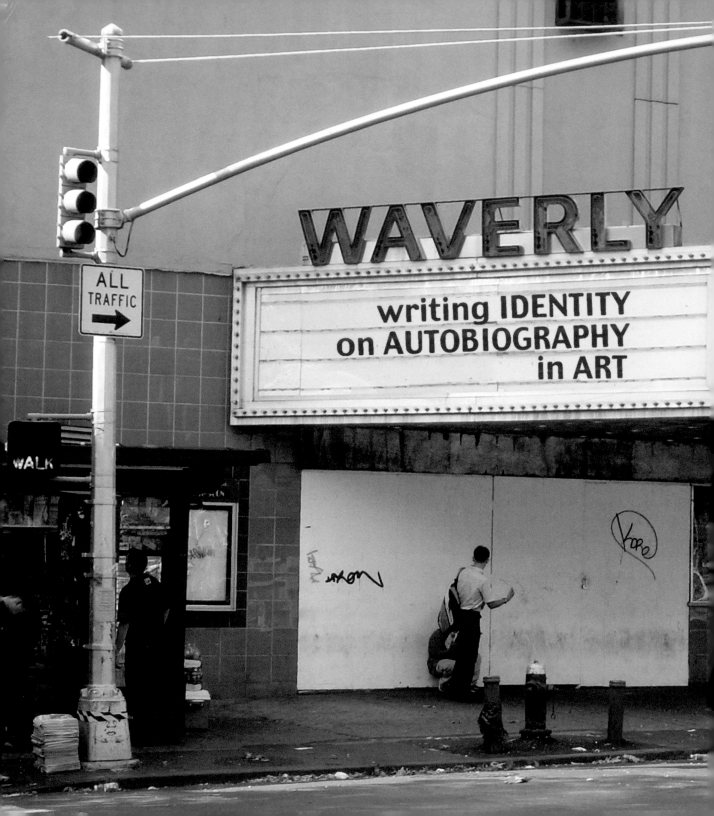

WRITING IDENTITY: ON AUTOBIOGRAPHY IN ART

The photo album and the autobiography are both by nature amateur activities, doomed from the outset to be failures and second-rate. For in arranging photos in an album, we are guided by the unconscious desire to show life in all its variety, and the result is the reduction of life to a series of dead fragments. Autobiography has a similar problem with the mechanics of memory: it is concerned with something that used to be, but it is written by someone who exists now.

Dubravka Ugrešić, *The Museum of Unconditional Surrender*, 1996

Every attempt to write — or claim to have written — a seamless narrative of a real life is doomed to failure. Conscious or unconscious gaps in memory demand to be bridged, and the result is an unending clash between the person who experienced and acted out the life of the past and the person now narrating and reflecting in the present. The control mechanisms of the psyche play an extraordinarily powerful part in blocking out unpleasant events and experiences – correcting, suppressing or glossing them over. Autobiographical narration typically displays a good deal of omission and interpretation, situating it somewhere between real events and the embellishments or supplements of memory. Furthermore, autobiographical texts are prefigured by the various literary modes and models of expression upon which their authors inevitably draw. These models in turn owe their existence to particular conventions and social contexts. Writing autobiography can, in the broadest sense, be viewed as a 'cultural technique of self-depiction and self-assurance'.[1] But even this is subject to change, for ideas of what is actually meant by the self have varied and still do vary considerably. They range from an imaginary coherent and autonomous self to one that is composed of many fragments – an idea of self that relieves the autobiographer of the need

opposite
Waverly
Jun Yang, 2002

to tell their whole life story. Thus the works presented here concentrate on extracts, periods, childhood and/or adulthood, or on significant individual experiences.

The history of autobiography

As most autobiographers use either spoken or written language, and consequently often draw on models from the history of literature, life stories are primarily seen and studied as a literary genre.[2] Most theoretical research on the subject has therefore been done under the umbrella of literary rather than art history. Autobiography narrated through pictures, or through a combination of pictures and text, tends to be restricted to monographs on individual artists,

Ideas of what is actually meant by the self have varied and still do vary considerably

and there is no systematic art-historical concept of the genre. But even literary research on autobiography is a relatively modern discipline; not until the beginning of the twentieth century do we find critical studies of particular autobiographies, although the genre of autobiography stretches back through the Middle Ages as far as Antiquity. It has occupied a special place since the late seventeenth century, when individual self-awareness slowly became a cultural point of focus.[3] In the eighteenth and nineteenth centuries, not only were there a number of extremely important autobiographies written, but their sheer quantity increased dramatically. It is therefore hardly surprising that at the beginning

of the twentieth century – when research on the subject really got under way – the history of autobiography was viewed primarily as a history of human self-awareness.[4] Some years later, closer attention began to be paid to personal documents as primary historical sources.[5] The expansion of civil institutions connected with education, health and security was not insignificant in the development of autobiography, even if for the most part their requirements were for potted histories rather than anything with literary pretensions.[6] Writing a report of oneself and one's life became historically a means of developing quantitative and qualitative norms of behaviour – the individual could be defined and disciplined on the basis of his or her own written account. But if on the one hand biographical data were a means by which institutions were able to exert social control, autobiographical writings could also draw attention to abuses and point the way towards social rebellion. This was true of women's autobiographical writings during the eighteenth and nineteenth centuries, which frequently were explicitly written to provide emancipatory models for other women to follow.[7]

The function, mode and, above all, literary status of autobiography have changed radically over the years. During the 1950s literary critics began to focus on the 'inner unity' of a work of autobiography, as distinct from other forms of self-documentation, such as diaries, letters, memoirs, etc.[8] Autobiographies were regarded as literary works of art if they evinced an 'aesthetic harmony of events, reflections, style and character.'[9] It was not until the 1970s that a growing interest in different autobiographical forms brushed aside this particular set of criteria. This partly came about through the growth of social history, which led to a new focus on the autobiographies of people from minorities and marginalized groups, in which they described their social rise along with their personal

The function, mode and, above all, literary status of autobiography have changed radically over the years

search for identity. But a great deal of attention was also now paid to questions of form. Critics studied the relationship between reader and autobiographer. Philippe Lejeune, for instance, spoke of a '*pacte autobiographique*' in which a trinity of identities had to be established for and accepted by the reader: those of the author, the narrator and the protagonist.[10] The concept of the unified, narrative life story became increasingly shaky from then onwards. The focus shifted from the evidence of an achieved identity, and the path that led to it, to the process of autobiographical writing itself as the arena in which the subject searches for identity, or rather for what is merely the possibility of an identity. This in turn was accompanied by a major change in the concept of the self. Gisela Brinkler-Gabler distinguishes between the universal, unified, developing self of traditional autobiography and the romantic, discursive self, suffused with internal 'oppositions'.[11] Kay Goodman, referring to female autobiography, speaks of the 'dispersed subject'.[12] But whether 'unified' or

'dispersed', the self is quite clearly an ideological construct, formulated and manifested in particular historical circumstances.

These shifts in the concepts of identity and self have been accompanied by a re-evaluation of women's autobiographies in particular, hitherto often dismissed as 'incomplete', 'discontinuous', 'incoherent', 'fragmentary' or 'private' – all because the life experiences they related did not touch upon what were considered to be the central social and political themes.[13] The new concept of the self and the increasing dissolution of fixed categories within the genre have resulted in interest shifting onto the process of writing autobiography, rather than the characteristics of the genre, for, in the words of Barbara Becker-Cantarino, 'A valid system for the genre of autobiography cannot be established for *all* literatures and *all* periods.'[14] Equally, the confinement

Whether 'unified' or 'dispersed', the self is quite clearly an ideological construct, formulated and manifested in particular historical circumstances

of autobiographical studies to the field of literature is also questionable. If coherent, continuous autobiographical narrative is an impossibility, then it makes sense to open up the study of autobiography to other forms of expression, just as the visual arts have, again since the 1970s, turned more and more towards other genres and disciplines.

Roberta
shman, 1976

Constructing Roberta Breitmore   *Lynn Hershman 1975*
(1) Lighten with Dior eyestick light (2) "Peach Blush" Cheekcolor by
Revlon. (3) Brown contour makeup by Coty. (4) Shape lips with brush,
fill in with "Date Mate" scarlet. 5. Blond wig (6) Ultra Blue eye-
shadow by Max Factor. (7) Maybelline black liner top and bottom
(8) $7.98 three piece dress. (9) Creme Beige liquid makeup by Artmatic.

The autobiographical subject

The most recent discussions of autobiography focus mainly on questions of the self and on the function of autobiographical writing in relation to establishing identity. In the context of changes in the very concepts of self and identity the actual term 'autobiography' is itself open to attack. New ideas are being mooted, especially in gender studies, with Domna Stanton, for instance, advocating the use of 'female autograph'[15] rather than 'autobiographer', for that term lays too much emphasis on the narration of one life, at the expense of the multiple, discontinuous elements of the

Autobiographers observe themselves, and open themselves up to observation by their readers. The process equates with looking in a mirror

typical female life. Even 'auto' seems questionable in the light of changing views of the self, since it suggests a unified and autonomous entity, thereby ignoring the 'socialization' of the subject. The French artist Christian Boltanski goes even further and maintains that 'there is no such thing as an autobiography'. He argues that 'the really interesting autobiographies are those that speak not of the author but of every reader'. As an example, he cites Proust: 'If you like Proust, it's because he does not speak so much about himself as about all of us – we have all been afraid of the dark and wished that our mother would say goodnight to us, and we've all been jealous, and we've all had a pretty daft great-aunt who we were fond of.'[16]

Here he is pointing to the central role of the reader, who from the very beginning is not only the all-important addressee of the author's words, but also the sharer of common social and cultural experiences with that author.

Nonetheless, this book retains the term 'autobiography', in spite of the survival of some of its outmoded meanings. The genre of autobiography has always been a melting-pot for various forms and modes of life story, even as the idea of the self has changed over the years. In other words, it must be seen as a variable and adaptable term that both embraces and transcends the genre, taking on new senses and constantly adjusting its focus according to the current demands of the writer, the person concerned and the public.

Let us now return to the special nature of autobiography, in which the writer is his or her own subject. Autobiographers observe themselves, and open themselves up to observation by their readers. The process equates with looking in a mirror, which according to Jacques Lacan plays an important part in the formation of the self.[17] Looking in the mirror, just like being looked at by society, is a means of constituting and identifying the self.[18] Lacan argues that this always localizes the image of the self in an exterior.[19] The formation of the self is a consecutive process: at one moment I am a subject, and then I am an object. This process is paralleled in the creation of autobiography, which allows one to see oneself as *someone else*, while the writing itself becomes a means of fashioning identity, and must be seen as the setting for the individual writer's formation of self. This concept of identity is quite different from the one that underlay earlier autobiographical research, whose starting-point was the assumption of a fully formed identity – a completed self, looking back on how it was shaped over the years. Now identity must be seen as contingent and forever incomplete, continually changing as it generates and regenerates itself. Thus to write an autobiography means, in essence, to write one's own identity.

Autobiography in art

Autobiography in art has certain features in common with the literary autobiography. Both claim a link between the narrating subject (the author), the life or episode of a life described, and the work that describes it. The first-person narrator remembers his or her life, or sections of it, and sets out to say something about it, even if this something is merely a brief description or just a reference. It may be that certain segments of a life appear only in the context of historical or social events, or are highlighted selectively. Such autobiography may well consist of fragments or sketches, and these may be arranged incoherently, without any overriding pattern or context.

This description fits the majority of the art works in this book. The border between fact and fiction is as fluid in the visual arts as it is in literature, and most of the time it is impossible to prove which is which, but even regardless of this, the very process of looking back over time must automatically result in distortions of reality. Nevertheless, although no autobiography can claim to be 'the truth', an author will conventionally aspire to a convincing approximation of truth. Some of the artists here deliberately throw open to question this very intention, building into their (partial) depiction of life clear pointers to its own fictionality. This marks a basic difference between the art works presented here and the majority of literary autobiographies, in which the 'desire for truth' is traditionally a defining criterion.[20]

The question of which identities are assumed in which autobiographical works becomes extremely complex with those artists who have created one or more different characters or alter egos through whom they speak or act. As we have already noted, seeing oneself as *someone else* is inherent in the process of creating any autobiography, but for such artists as Eleanor Antin, Lynn Hershman and Anita Leisz it is the very substance of their work. When Eleanor Antin depicts herself in the guise of 'The Angel of Mercy', 'The Nurse' or 'The King', she assumes real but contradictory male and female roles – as a caring, socially active woman or as a male ruler – and so subjects herself to different social conditions and responses. Antin equips each of her alter egos with their own biography, which intersects with her biography. She thus lays bare not only the fictional nature of her characters, but also that of her own and everyone else's biographical story. Lynn Hershman works along similar lines: the invented character Roberta Breitmore lives her 'own' life for several years. She has her own credit cards and bank account, visits a psychiatrist, attends Weight Watchers, writes in her

**A territory to be mastered
in the same as patagonia**
Elke Krystufck, 2001

own handwriting, has her own flat and clothes. When Roberta advertises for a maid and real people respond, she becomes 'part of her own reality' and this reality is a 'component of her fiction'.[21] Just how much Roberta is to be identified with Hershman we do not know. And perhaps neither does Hershman, for whom 'Roberta's traumas [became her] own … tormenting memories'.[22] While Lynn Hershman creates female alter egos, Anita Leisz gives herself a male identity. Initially conceived as a comic-strip character, 'Den Rest' is not only Anita's virtual companion, but his life also merges with hers for long periods. He follows through 'the rest' of those plans that have got left behind in Anita's own life; or he takes up options that were not open to her in the first place, or that she would not have wanted to have open to her. The process in which the autobiographer sees him or herself as 'other', usually only implicit, is made explicit in these alter egos. And at the same time, each artist's own autobiographical story becomes as porous, fragmented and constructed as that of their fictional 'other' selves.

There are many other artists – such as Andy Warhol, Jeff Koons, Cindy Sherman and Christian Boltanksi – who are equally intangible autobiographically. Warhol cultivated himself as pure surface which could be played upon at will. He deliberately extinguished his own self and story, and subjected himself to a variety of projections that fell on his person from outside and, as it were, wrote themselves upon him. Koons, on the other hand, assumes the persona of the smart and successful artist right from the start, and develops this image through the years, much to his advantage in terms of publicity and financial reward. His self-depiction is thus devoted mainly to promoting his own 'designer' personality. His scandal-laden marriage to former porn star Ilona Staller gets the full commercial treatment, while his artistic career is presented as truly exemplary. Public appearances and well-staged interviews cleverly nourish public interest in his *real life*, and the 'Jeff Koons' brand becomes a perfect product with its own appropriate biography.

Krassimir Krastev also seeks to embody the perfect brand – not in his case that of the smart artist-entrepreneur like Koons, but that of the playboy sportsman, an iconic figure in his homeland of Bulgaria. Under the trademark RASSIM®, he displays his muscular, well-developed body in videos, on posters, and as statuesque cardboard cutouts. His path to this perfection is fully documented: we follow the complete transformation from a smoking artist to a sporting idol. The 'real' Krastev disappears behind a brand name and an exaggerated musculature. In her *Untitled Film Stills*, Cindy Sherman continually slips into different roles and female stereotypes drawn and staged from the history of cinema, and by doing so she not only denies them their identity, but she also conceals her own. Sherman stresses that the *Untitled Film Stills* are not about her personally; she merely uses herself as her material.[23] But in the endless role-playing, the possibility of coherent individual biography dissolves.

> Warhol cultivated himself as pure surface which could be played upon at will. He deliberately extinguished his own self and story

In a number of works of the 1960s and 1970s, Christian Boltanski repeatedly set out to reconstruct his life. He often did this, however, by introducing 'foreign' material or by manufacturing scenes. In *Portrait Photographs of C.B.*, for example, fictitious documents and photos of friends or of strangers 'illustrate' his life story. Photographs of anonymous boys of different ages invoke Boltanski's own childhood years. He 'deduces' his autobiography from accepted ideas of childhood and collective memories, reconstructing it by relating himself to the lives of others. On Kawara and Mary Kelly opt for a purely factual reconstruction of their lives, or of extracts from their lives. Kawara draws up a precise list of unadorned facts which accumulate into a detailed account. In *I met*, *I read*, *I went*, he arranges events under different categories, thereby tracing the various trajectories of his life and at the same time confirming his existence. The subjective adjustments of hindsight and interpretation are scrupulously avoided.

Kelly's *Post-Partum Document* takes the birth of her child – traditionally a key event in female autobiographies – as the starting-point for a detailed list of her own data and those of the child. Although Kawara and Kelly use various systems to record their facts, the archival principle is common to both. Kawara's documentation of basic activities and confirmation of his own existence, like Kelly's record of an all-important period of her life, is extremely compressed, dealing only with repeated daily activities. However, while Kawara dispenses with all comments, anecdotes or references that are not purely factual, Kelly appends her factual records with personal observations and emotions. She deliberately allows the subjective to intrude.

The tension between objective and subjective, public and private, is also a feature of Gerhard Richter's work *Atlas*. Compiled over many years, this began as a collection of amateur snapshots and cuttings from newspapers and magazines, which both mirror the outside world[24] and reveal Richter's artistic interests and preoccupations. But in time he started to include images documenting important events in his own life, such as his relationships and the birth of his child. This positioning of his own autobiography alongside outside events has the effect both of making those public events part of his private story, and bestowing universal significance upon private subject matter.

At first glance, Elke Krystufek appears to assert the possibility, indeed the primacy, of authentic personal expression. Through her paintings, videos and performances she seems to be offering the most intimate and personal revelations of her self. But upon closer inspection these turn out to be always more or less stereotypical, based on conventional roles and behaviours. When Krystufek says that she would like to be 'authentic',[25] she is recognizing the impossibility of this aspiration, and expressing her own unfulfillable desire.

On Kawara draws up a precise list of unadorned facts which accumulate into a detailed account. The subjective adjustments of hindsight and interpretation are scrupulously avoided

Tracey Emin also appears to make no distinction between her private and her artistic life. For *Everyone I Have Ever Slept With 1963–1995*, she stitched on the inside of a tent the names of all her sleeping partners: these range from childhood friends through to lovers. Other stories are so intimate they give the impression that they simply must be true. She talks about alcoholism, rape, betrayal, and openly confesses her private 'faults'. But this private self is always staged in public, displayed at exhibitions and in other public places. As with Sophie Calle's seemingly authentic photographic and textual records of her life, what is 'real' and what is a performance staged for the benefit of the viewer, or the camera, remains open to question.

Antje Schiffers's work also questions the possibility of an authentic report. On her return from journeys to Cixa Huaxtla in Mexico, for example, or Kazakhstan, or Kirghizia, she uses writing, painting and drawing to describe her experiences and adventures in foreign countries, as well as to depict the people she encountered. On her travels, she employs her talents as an artist with the deliberate aim of starting conversations and building relationships with people, who often initially treat her with a mixture of suspicion and curiosity, which soften in a gradual rapprochement. In the process, her own autobiography, opinions and attitudes continually intersect with those of the people she meets, so that during these journeys Schiffers's identity is both dependent upon and sidelined by her meetings with other people.

Christine Hill's autobiography is embodied in the success story of her *Volksboutique* project, which in turn is the story of her artistic career. She set up the first 'office' of the *Volksboutique* in her birthplace of Binghamton, New York. After a period in Baltimore, where she was a student, and following a lengthy stay in Berlin, where she set up and ran the *Volksboutique* second-hand clothing store, Hill's 'home office' migrated to Brooklyn, New York, supplemented by temporary 'mobile offices' set up in different locations as required. The changing phases and locations of her life thus provide a framework for her artistic project. *Volksboutique* has become an artistic brand that Hill defines and promotes by drawing parallels with the 'dishwasher to millionaire' success myths of American heroes like Steven Forbes or Bill Gates.

Jun Yang, Anny and Sibel Öztürk, TOBIAS Z. and Rirkrit Tiravanija all grew up between two or more cultures. As with so many second-generation immigrants, the knowledge they have of the origins and cultural backgrounds of their families consists of a patchwork of vague memories, tales told by their parents and grandparents, brief visits, and films.

This reliance on second-hand experience means that their autobiographical works use what amount to cultural set-pieces in order to (re)construct their own identity. Their concept of their 'own' culture is sometimes no less of a cliché than the mental and media images that are in everyday circulation. Expectations of ethnicity are also an explicit theme in the work of Adrian Piper and Shirana Shahbazi. As a woman, an artist and a black person, Piper takes up her position in an ideological field which embraces

For so many second-generation immigrants, the knowledge they have of the cultural backgrounds of their families consists of a patchwork of vague memories, tales told by their parents and grandparents, brief visits, and films

the political, the economic, the sociological and the cultural, and which also to a large extent predetermines the scope of her social activity. Her own person and her life story form the starting-point of her theoretical and practical analyses. In her *Context* works of the early 1970s, Piper refuted the idea of the autonomy of art by gathering together material that served as evidence of her dependence on the norms and networks of society, then exhibiting it in the form of files in those very institutions that proclaim the autonomy of art. In *Funk Lessons*, she teaches white Americans how to dance to Afro-American music after she herself has been repeatedly confronted with stereotypes of African music and dance.

Photographer Shirana Shahbazi's own origins were not originally in the foreground of her art, and it was only the way that her work was received that caused her to turn the focus onto her own biography: the daughter

Shahbazi positions her work between her own autobiography and the images that others project onto her from outside

of an Iranian in Germany, she is an artist who has lived in Europe for years, with a Swiss husband. These facts, and the preconceptions they invoke, are inseparable from the reception of her work, which she positions between her own autobiography and the images that others project onto her from outside. Thus her own photographs and those she commissions contain features that confirm the stereotypes of life in an Islamic country, but they are counterbalanced by other features that are equally stereotypical of the western or American way of life. The closer you look, the more contrasts and borderlines disappear and everything merges.

The tense political situation in South Africa is the background to William Kentridge's work, which faces up critically to the various developments in that troubled land. Man's increasing brutality towards his fellow beings as well as towards nature during apartheid, and the desperate search for social balance after the abolition of apartheid – these are constant themes in Kentridge's films and drawings, in which biography and politics continually impinge on one another. Two of his most recurrent characters – Soho Eckstein, a capitalist building contractor, and the dreamer Felix – can certainly be viewed as autobiographical figures: the former bears a resemblance to Morris Kentridge, the artist's grandfather, and Felix is not unlike the artist himself, although the characters are also a mixture of each.

Tracey Rose's starting-point is also the repressive apartheid system in South Africa. As a woman of mixed race, she grew up categorized as a 'coloured person', a half-way status between white and black. This formative experience of being in an indeterminate position in the social order is what drives her work. Rose takes on various roles and tests them as potential for identity. She changes from white to black, female to male, as she acts out stock characters such as Lolita, the nun or the pin-up.

The Soviet state with its communal institutions, symbols and rituals are recurrent themes in Ilya Kabakov's work, in which public events and personal experiences constantly intersect. In his installations, such as *Communal Living*, he is usually present indirectly through photographs, autobiographical texts or personal belongings. The effect is to evoke a continual

tension between his life and its social framework –
a system which he did not choose to live under, but
which impinges on his personal freedom of choice.

Similarly Johannes Wohnseifer draws his creative ideas
from existing historical, political and cultural sources,
producing a body of work that traces both a personal
and a collective history. Brands, events and individuals
– Braun, Adidas, Rainer Fassbinder, RAF, Honda,
Otl Aicher, the 1972 Munich Olympics – all of these
and more feature in his work. By incorporating the
political events, celebrities, religious objects and
contemporary icons that have signposted the path
from his childhood through to the present, he causes
his own history to merge indistinguishably from that
of West Germany.

Autobiography and social conditions are inextricably
bound together in the work of Johanna Kandl, too.
She was born in 1954 in Vienna, and grew up in a part
of the city that was occupied by the Soviet Union for
the decade from 1945 to 1955. Stories and pictures of
this period fascinated her from an early age. Many
years later, for her 'Wünsdorf Project', she followed the
withdrawal of Russian troops from the Soviet garrison
in the former East Germany, and their resettlement
north-west of Moscow. Her snapshots formed the
basis of a series of paintings in which she reflects and
comments on these political, economic and social
events, which impinge on her own personal story.

The work of Oliver Musovik and Anri Sala deals with
processes of social change in southeast Europe. Both

top
[Dokhtar-07-2002]
from 'Goftare Nik/Good Words'
Shirana Shahbazi, 2000–2

[Tehran-09-2002]
from 'Goftare Nik/Good Words'
Shirana Shahbazi, 2000–2

Johannesburg, Second Greatest City after Paris
William Kentridge, 1989

of them begin with their immediate environment: Musovik deals with family, friends and neighbours, while Sala is concerned with his own family history. Musovik was born in Macedonia, which used to be part of the Federal Republic of Yugoslavia, and he still lives in Skopje. The views he offers of his own everyday life provide insights into the social upheavals

that touch everyone in this transitional post-Communist state. While Musovik concentrates on the political, economic and social present as framed by his own personal life, Sala goes back into the past. In *Intervista*, he exposes the political involvement of his mother in the former Communist regime. The story of his mother is part of his own story and that of the Albanian nation too.

Dorit Margreiter, Ruby Sircar and Rosemarie Trockel all focus on the influence of cinematic and media images on the building of individual identity. Both Margreiter and Sircar come from hybrid cultural backgrounds: Margreiter is Chinese-Austrian, Sircar is Indian-German. Margreiter examines the part played by soap operas in shaping the daily reality of her friends and relatives, while Sircar looks to the enormous impact of Hindi and Bollywood films on second-generation immigrants from the Indian subcontinent. The German artist Trockel looks further back in the past, to the early explosion of the mass media in the 1950s and 1960s. She explores the emancipatory influence of Brigitte Bardot on a whole generation of young girls, including herself, through Bardot's extensive magazine exposure. Margreiter and Sircar share this interest in women's emancipation, and in the way that women are depicted. In *@mp (asiatic mode of production)* Sircar examines a number of different films and the ways in which they confirm or defy the traditional limits of women's roles, and in this context she also examines their influence on her own life story. Margreiter asked her Chinese mother to read Boye De Mente's cliché-laden

Tea and coffee in the grass between Paris House and Antenor House. Ruta from Lithuania looks at photos – we did in Vilnius some years ago. She lives here in London since a few month. Her daughter – Ruta speaks English already very fluently.

In the afternoon on Saturday, 15 th of August, 1998.

Untitled (Tea and Coffee...)
Johanna Kandl, 1999

but widely read 1992 book *Women of the Orient: Intimate Profiles of the World's Most Feminine Women*. Her video, also titled *Women of the Orient*, records her mother calmly reading aloud De Mente's absurd statements about the 'nature' of Asian women. Margreiter emphasizes the constructed, fictive quality of his assertions by presenting the project as a movie featuring Elaine Tak Yee Margreiter (her mother), with camerawork and editing credited to herself.

Kubelka delivers a kind of daily report on her own state of mind, and the unending reformulation of her identity

Friedl Kubelka's pictorial autobiography shows her continually questioning and re-identifying herself. Almost every day for a whole year she studied and recorded her own facial expression, with all its changing moods and emotions, thereby delivering a kind of daily report on her own state of mind, and the unending reformulation of her identity. Through a number of different projects, Moira Zoitl also investigates processes of identity formation – her own and that of other women. In *I was 0.doc* she reconstructs the notorious 'Lady's Room' which the Viennese architect Adolf Loos built for one of his clients. Loos's architecture reduced its female occupant to the role of housewife and mother, confining her to the domestic world and so perpetuating the mechanics of sexual repression. Into this setting, Zoitl places a video which replays her life from birth to the age of twenty through anecdotes and reminiscences. The

video recounts how she gradually escaped from the controlling and defining powers of her mother and family, and so achieved independence. Zoitl thus subverts the repressive agenda of Loos's architecture, using it to make a feminist statement and to assert her own emancipation.

Nan Goldin's starting-point is also the contingency of identity. She photographs friends and acquaintances, many of whom have 'overstepped the narrow sexual boundaries' of mainstream society[26] – transsexuals, drag queens and transvestites, people who either cannot or will not decide on their own sexual identity. Goldin's photographs follow the lives of her friends, and in so doing reflect Goldin's own life, too, and the period that she lived among them.

Childhood memories form the basis of Wiebke Loeper's work. *MOLL 31* is devoted to the history of her own family and their life in a prefabricated concrete *Plattenbau*. She juxtaposes photos taken by her father in the 1970s with her own of thirty years later. In *Lad* she seeks out scenes of her childhood in East Berlin – her school, the playground, the department store – photographs them, and appends her comments. She studies these places, which were once of such importance to her, with a view to assessing their influence on her identity. But this can only be partially successful: memory stumbles over the concreteness of the settings, which themselves coagulate into mere pictures. As she says, 'The place which houses childhood memories, and to which I could return in order to feed off its substance, disappears.'[27]

Just as autobiographies must always remain incomplete, so this book cannot claim completeness. But what the diverse approaches it presents all have in common is their scepticism towards the possibility of an authentic, coherent life story. Autobiography is the product of various factors – real experiences, together with things heard, seen, read, narrated and invented. Fact and fiction are inextricably woven together. The image introducing this essay shows the old Waverly Cinema

Autobiography is the product of various factors – real experiences, together with things heard, seen, read, narrated and invented. Fact and fiction are inextricably woven together

in New York, closed for many years and now only accessible by way of memory a relic of former times. It forms a perfect surface on which to project images of both the past and the present. It also, appropriately, introduces the idea of film, for the parallel between autobiographical narration and film is one that recurs throughout this book. This old cinema symbolizes for us the interweaving of identity and autobiography, of fact and fiction, of past and present.

Notes

1 Von Engelhardt, Michael, 'Geschlechtsspezifische Muster des mündlichen autobiographischen Erzählens im 20. Jahrhundert', in: Magdalene Heuser, *Autobiographien von Frauen: Beiträge zu ihrer Geschichte*, Tübingen, 1996, 369

2 On the history of autobiography in literature, see Günter Niggl, *Die Autobiographie: Zu Form und Geschichte einer literarischen Gattung*, Wissenschaftliche Buchgesellschaft, Darmstadt, 1998

3 Von Engelhardt, op. cit., 369

4 Misch, Georg, 'Begriff und Ursprung der Autobiographie' (1907/1949), in: Niggl (ed.), op. cit.

5 Mahrholz, Werner, 'Der Wert der Selbstbiographie als geschichtliche Quelle' (1919), in: Niggl (ed.), op. cit.

6 The institutional demand for short biographies should be seen here in the context of Michel Foucault's observations on the disciplinary powers of institutions (Foucault [1976] 1992). See also Von Engelhardt (op. cit., 369 f), who draws attention to the massive number of personal writings during the nineteenth century.

7 Heuser, Magdalene, 'Einleitung' [Introduction], in: Heuser, op. cit.

8 Shumaker, Wayne, 'Die englische Autobiographie: Gestalt und Aufbau' (1954), in: Niggl (ed.), op. cit.

9 Gusdorf, George, 'Voraussetzungen und Grenzen der Autobiographie' (1956) and Pascal, Roy, 'Die Autobiographie als Kunstform' (1959), both in: Niggl (ed.), op. cit.

10 Lejeune, Philippe, 'Der autobiographische Pakt' (1973/75), Frankfurt am Main, 1994

11 Brinkler-Gabler, Gisela, 'Metamorphosen des Subjekts: Autobiographie, Textualität und Erinnerung', in: Heuser, op. cit., 395

12 Goodman, Kay, 'Weibliche Autobiographien', in: Hiltrud Gnüg and Renate Möhrmann, *Frauen Literatur Geschichte*, Stuttgart, 1985. According to Goodman, the fragmentary female subject has already been revealed by research on women's autobiographies around 1800. Goodman contrasts this fragmented, split self with the unified self to be found in male autobiographies written at the same time.

13 Magdalene Heuser argues that even if 'interest in autobiographies / autobiographical writing / first-person documents has increased dramatically', and there is now a 'rich and fertile body of research work', women's autobiographies would still 'at best be marginalised or otherwise ignored altogether, even in modern times' (Heuser, op. cit., 1). It was not until 1986 that Eda Sagarra's voluminous bibliography of women's autobiographical works gave a kick-start to research into this field.

14 Becker-Cantarino, Barbara, '"Erwählung des besseren Teils": Zur Problematik von Selbstbild und Fremdbild in Anna Maria van Schurmans "Eukleria"' (1973), in: Heuser, op. cit., 27

15 Stanton, Domna, *The Female Autograph: Theory and Practice of Autobiography from the Tenth to the Twentieth Century*, Chicago and London, 1987, VII

16 Boltanski, Christian, *Inventar* (exh. cat.), Hamburger Kunsthalle, Hamburg, 1991, 57

17 According to Lacan, the mother also plays an important part in the early stages of the self's formation.

18 When looking in the mirror, the child sees itself as (or mistakes itself for) an entity. This fiction leads to a split in the self between 'je' and 'moi', with 'moi' standing for the idea of unity, while 'je' stands for the experience of not conforming to this idea. The mirror image is viewed as a rival, because it possesses a completeness which the 'je' desires but cannot achieve. After overcoming this mirror phase, the self enters into the 'symbolic' or social order to which all human consciousness is subject. Through language the self learns to symbolize its needs and to free itself from its physical immediacy (see Lacan, Jacques, 'Das Spiegelstadium als Bildner der Ich-Funktion, wie sie uns in der psychoanalytischen Erfahrung erscheint' [1949], in: Norbert Haas [ed.], *Schriften I*, Weinheim, Berlin, 1996, 61–70).

19 'Basically, the visible me is determined by the look that is outside me' (Lacan, Jacques, 'Das Subjekt und der/das Andere', in: Norbert Haas and Hans Joachim Metzger [eds], *Die vier Grundbegriffe der Psychoanalyse* [1964], *Das Seminar*, Buch IX, Weinheim, Berlin, 1996, 113)

20 Aichinger, Ingrid, 'Probleme der Autobiographie als Sprachkunstwerk' (1970), in: Niggl (ed.), op. cit., 183

21 Lynn Hershman in e-mail to authors, 2002

22 ibid.

23 Neven Du Mont, Gisela, and Dickhoff, Wilfried (eds), *Cindy Sherman*, Cologne, 1995, 15

24 Friedel, Helmut, in: Sabine Breitwieser (ed.), *Double Life: Identität und Transformation in der Zeitgenössischen Kunst*, Generali Foundation (exh. cat.), Vienna, 2001

25 Elke Krystufek in e-mail to authors, 2002

26 Goldin, Nan, *The Other Side*, New York, Zurich and Berlin, 1992, 6

27 Loeper, Wiebke, *Lad* (exh. cat.), Künstlerhaus Bethanien, Berlin, 2001

ALTER EGO

If autobiography is made, even made up, rather than given, does that make it closer to fiction than to fact? These artists invent characters and enact their stories, or weave those characters' stories in and out of their own. Where does the real finish and the invented begin?

Between 1973 and 1978, American artist Lynn Hershman played the invented character of Roberta Breitmore. Hershman gave Roberta a life of her own, independent of the artist's, with her own apartment, credit card, bank account, signature, and so on. She recorded Roberta's real day-to-day experiences, such as going to the psychiatrist (opposite) or meeting a man in a park who had answered an ad she placed looking for a roommate. Through Roberta's life story, Hershman was able to explore a number of feminist issues, such as the way society constructs women's identities, and how women become victims of the structures and conditioning imposed upon them.

Hershman, who now works mainly in the digital realm, has long produced art with an interactive element. Her interactive video disk *Lorna* (1982), about a woman so terrified by what she sees on television that she is afraid to leave her hotel room, invited viewers/ participants to eavesdrop on the woman's telephone conversations, her only connection to the outside world. They could also link to stories about her past and decide her future. Depending on which ending participants select, Lorna shoots her TV, commits suicide, or – most frightening of all – moves to Los Angeles. Like the works by Hershman shown here, this piece is about how autobiography is made, or even made up, rather than given, and how it can appear different from different people's viewpoints.

top
Roberta Meets I
Lynn Hershman, 1976

Multiples
Lynn Hershman, 1976

'Every autobiography is concerned with two characters, a Don Quixote, the Ego, and a Sancho Panza, the Self.'
W. H. Auden

Psychiatric Sessions
Lynn Hershman, 1976

'Roberta's childhood and background were predefined. Her behaviours stemmed from the early traumas of her simulated history, which began in 1971 when she arrived, via a Greyhound bus, in San Francisco and checked into the Dante Hotel. The desolate, lonely room in the Dante Hotel and the intrinsic collected symbols of identity gestated into the fictional persona of Roberta. They, like Roberta's ephemeral nature, were a framing device for the ways in which ambiguous objects signify character.'
Lynn Hershman

rinde eckertx2

rachel rosenthal

irtual, electronic, seeing!!!believeir

kathy acker

Guillermo Gomez Pena

who am I? Where do I come from?

we become what we do,
we are what we believe =
diaries, autobiography, life

The Electronic Diaries
Lynn Hershman, 1984

**The Electronic Diaries:
First Person Plural**
Lynn Hershman, 1984

Since 1984 Hershman has produced *The Electronic Diaries*, a three-part video series constituting the on-going diary of an individual, performed by the artist, who tells her story of sexual and physical abuse through a series of personal narratives. The videos record the transformation of the character as her story unfolds and include interviews with the artist's friends, who add their own personal experiences of pain, making connections between childhood trauma and violent historical events. The piece is about — as Hershman puts it — 'ageing and the delusions and misperceptions we are encumbered with as we mature towards self-awareness'.

'The diary has long been a way for women to record private thoughts. Told in [the] first person, this video diary reveals both my reaction to culture, as well as formally, through electronic techniques, mirroring the fracturing, rupturing, obsessive and alienating trauma and dreams we, members of this society, share. Individuals reflect their culture, and can not be separated from it.... It was during the making of these tapes that I remembered my own historical trauma, became angry that my lack of esteem, guilt and disabilities were all part of my having been an unwitting victim. On camera, that realization itself brought consciousness, and ultimately the ability to transcend my personal history.'
Lynn Hershman

'I am interested in defining the limits of myself, meaning moving out to, in to, up to, and down to the frontiers of myself.'

Eleanor Antin

For more than three decades, American artist Eleanor Antin has been at the forefront of women's performance art. Through the creation of invented personae, she playfully addresses serious questions about gender and the formation of female identity. The King was Antin's first alter ego and was created in 1972. The artist wanted to look at the 'other half of mankind', as she put it, and so wanted to become the perfect, idealized male self, which was represented for her by the archetypal (iconic) male figure of the king. A series of photographic portraits accompanied a video, which showed her gradual transformation into a man as she put on a beard. In a number of live performances, Antin walked through the streets of Solana Beach, a small beach town in north San Diego County, dressed as the town's monarch. During these performances, he/she greeted the King's subjects all around 'the kingdom'.

In 1973, Antin created another alter ego, the Ballerina, now representing her idealized female self. Antin wanted the Ballerina to stand not only for a dancer but 'for all creative types and aspirants to an ideal'. Whereas the photographs seem to depict a ballerina of great poise and refinement, the accompanying video (*Caught in the Act*) reveals her efforts to hold apparently perfect poses. Constantly falling, stumbling and losing her footing, she has to support herself with a broomstick or a hidden chair. In this way, Antin is playing someone who is trying to imitate her ideal but repeatedly fails. She wants to improve herself, to fulfil the image of perfection, but cannot.

The Ballerina
Eleanor Antin, 1974

The Nurse
Eleanor Antin, 1976

In 1976, Antin developed the persona of the Nurse, having observed that nursing was traditionally considered a field reserved for women and a perfect female service to mankind. In each of her 'Nurse' projects, she explored popular cultural clichés associated with nursing. In the feature-length movie *The Adventures of a Nurse*, Antin played both the narrator and the nurse, while all the other characters were paper dolls created and operated by the artist. A bed functioned as the stage. The central figure was Nurse Eleanor, who falls easily in love – first with a dying poet, then with a biker, a doctor, a French ski bum and an anti-war senator. Inevitably, the affairs lead to constant disappointment. In this work, Antin parodied not only the conventions of television soap operas but also the place and role of the caring woman in a male-dominated society.

'Role playing was about feeling that I didn't have a self. And I didn't miss it.... [But] I am in all my pieces, even if you don't see me.'
Eleanor Antin

A year later, Antin continued the nursing theme by creating the character 'Eleanor Nightingale', based on the life of Florence Nightingale, the founder of modern nursing. Under the title *The Angel of Mercy* she developed several photo-album projects. One, 'The Nightingale Family Album', documented the life of the Victorian, aristocratic Nightingale family at their country home outside London; another, 'My Tour of Duty in the Crimea', consisted of Eleanor Nightingale's view of life and death on the battlefield. The two albums complement each other. The photographs mimic the poses, fashions and attitudes of Victorian ladies and soldiers of war; the tinted gelatin silver prints are made to look old with stains, creases and scratches. In addition to the albums, Antin also wrote a play in two acts, which she performed with almost life-size cut-out figures derived from characters in the photographs.

The Angel of Mercy
Eleanor Antin, 1976–77

'[It] is a very curious type of autobiography, the depiction of a life, or part of a life, three weeks of a life that is both invention and fact, as all life is.'
Eleanor Antin

opposite and pages 40–43
Are those your relatives?
Anita Leisz, 2002

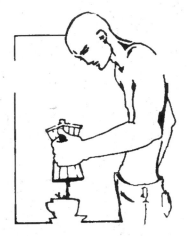

Den Rest
Anita Leisz, 1998

Den Rest
Anita Leisz, 1998

Austrian artist Anita Leisz created the comic-strip figure Den Rest (meaning 'The Rest', as in 'the rest of me') in the early 1990s as a virtual companion for herself. She equipped the character with his own life story, giving him a past, present and future, and the qualities, traits and ambitions she herself did not or could not possess – either because of her own personality or because of her sex. With Den Rest, Leisz is questioning the very possibility of presenting anyone's biography as an authentic whole, as a coherent narrative. She shows how life stories – whether one's own or someone else's – are always porous, fragmented and often disorientating. The narrative of Den Rest's life takes confusing twists and turns, jumping backwards and forwards in time or between people and places; Den plays other characters, and makes up events that never happened; at times his life seems to merge with the artist's.

The text and photo work on the following pages, *Are those your relatives?*, is an episode in Den's life: a conversation between him (here playing 'Daniel') and his friend René about René's family, who appear in photographs on his walls. His friend's account sounds genuine, even though he found or bought all the photos, and so his tales are fiction. All the time, Leisz is drawing attention to the fact that René's and Den's autobiographies – and by implication everyone's autobiographies – have been constructed, by inserting into the story details about where René got the photographs, for instance, or by naming herself as the author of the 'text' midway through.

daniel stood up to look at the photos on the wall next to the desk

are those your relatives?

yes, responded rené
daniel noticed that the photos had been framed and hung with great
care, that they look good together as a whole

is that your brother and his wife sitting by the window: the woman is
blonde and smiling and he has dark hair and looks to be about thirty,

and this?… he points to another photo … and waits … your parents?
he lifts his head: yes, those are my parents.

den goes back and lies next to him

that can't be, rené
what?
your parents.
they both have blue eyes
and your eyes are brown.

rené looks at him
you are right – those are not my parents

or they might have adopted you
yes –
no, they are not my adoptive parents
I do not know them.
you don't know them?
no
and your brother?
he is not my brother

but I also find that we look alike

daniel: den rest
rené: rené dessler
photos: couple sitting by the window: found september 1999 gartengasse, vienna
wedding party: bought for 50 cents at the vienna naschmarkt, may 2002
couple at the airport: bought for 2 euros, june 2002
text: anita leisz

so does your brother have a name
everyone has a name...

1969
iris carl crosses the square and greets her neighbour dora schneitel.
rushing by she calls:

happy new year ... and thinks: a good year
dora shakes her head

rené has another collection of photographs; photos of women
who were young in the sixties.

Children (from the series 'Picture This!')
Oliver Hangl, 2001

below
Lucky like Daniel Rose
Oliver Hangl, 1997

Oliver Hangl, also from Austria, originally started his career as an actor and stage designer. Working in a variety of different media, he operates at the point of intersection between theatre, cinema and the fine arts, and he frequently switches between the positions of artist, actor, producer and/or director. He denies any close autobiographical link with the fictional character he developed in 1994, Daniel Rose. In fact, what really interests him is the potential distance between himself and Daniel. Inspired by a Woody Allen film – in one scene, the hero emerges from a movie screen and becomes a reality for the character played by Mia Farrow – Hangl explores the borders between fact and fiction, their mutual influence, and the real-life consequences of fictional situations. The Daniel Rose character is also open to interpretation from others. In 1997–98 Hangl collaborated with the British artist Georgina Starr. In 1998 the Austrian painter Georg Wagenhuber did portraits of two versions of Daniel Rose, one played by the artist himself and the other by his friend, part-time actor Michael Krassnitzer.

'Every role is also influenced by real life. James Bond is different when he is played by Roger Moore instead of Sean Connery. Conversely, a role assumed over a short period of time can change real life.'
Oliver Hangl

Daniel Rose: shooting exercise
Oliver Hangl, 1996

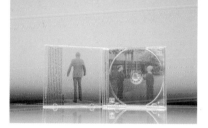

Mr Rose
Oliver Hangl, 2000

top centre and right
two timing 2
Oliver Hangl, 2002

above
Portrait of Daniel Rose
Georg Wagenhuber, 1998

'Starvision' (Danny Rose comic)
Georgina Starr, 1997

**Daniel Rose Museum 1
(installation view)**
Oliver Hangl, 1997

Daniel Rose from A–Z
Oliver Hangl, 1998

The Belgian artist Ria Pacquée first created the character of Madame in the 1980s. Just like Lynn Hershman (pages 30–33) and Eleanor Antin (pages 34–37), Pacquée herself plays the part of her invented character, who lacks any specific identity – unless her very identity is to have no identity. Madame is entirely average: she has a blank, expressionless face, blonde curled hair, big glasses, a large handbag, a pale raincoat (of sensible length) and practical shoes. We know very little about her life, aside from a few trips she has made, for instance to the National Garden Festival in Gateshead, the Cologne Carnival, and a pilgrimage to Lourdes. But in each of these places she is alone and inconspicuous within the crowd as she tries to catch a glimpse of a member of the British royal family (Gateshead), or hopes for a miracle (Lourdes). Madame, alias Ria Pacquée, could be anyone at all – and yet she is no one in particular. She is a person, but she cannot be captured biographically. Indeed, she seems almost too timid to assume a persona, or merit a biography. She is the ultimate average person and, at the same time, a non-person; she is everyone and no one. Her 'story' serves only to highlight the fact that she has no life story.

From the series 'Madame going on pilgrimage to Lourdes'
Ria Pacquée, 1989

opposite

From the series 'Madame at carnival in Cologne'
Ria Pacquée, 1989

'Disguised as an average woman of indeterminate age, I infiltrate real-life situations, which are discreetly captured by a photographer. In the role of Madame, I illustrate the loneliness and the emptiness of an everyday person. As a result of her unstable social situation and the way she leads her life completely aloof, she is just killing time. She personifies the masses.'

**From the series 'Madame goes
to see the horse racing show'**
Ria Pacquée, 1989

From the series 'The girl who was never asked to marry'
Ria Pacquée, 1988

DISAPPEARANCE

Many of us sometimes want to disappear. But are we trying to escape our past, or our present? Each of the artists here hides behind a mask, a persona or an invented identity in order to force attention away from their real lives, or else to vanish completely.

From 1942 until his death in 1987, Andy Warhol created a variety of different self-portraits. Like so much of his art, they claim value for pure surface: for Warhol, someone's personality is no more than a 'look', and it can be changed at will. Warhol was greatly inspired by fashion, which allows the individual to continually reinvent him- or herself. Several of his late self-portraits show his face covered with camouflage veils. His features disappear behind this familiar disguise; the colourful surface pattern becomes dominant.

Throughout his life Warhol was also attracted to drag culture, which found multiple expression in his work. In the early 1980s, he used heavy make-up and wigs as another form of disguise to transform himself into female-like personae. By mimicking the poses and features of female stars, he expressed a shift in gender, thereby erasing an aspect of his 'true' self and opening up the possibility of an alternative autobiography.

And yet, somewhat paradoxically, at the same time as Warhol was extinguishing himself with his art, he was also promoting himself as a highly visible brand – 'Andy Warhol' (page 55). And he was also preserving his life for posterity by filling 'time capsules' with the remains of his day-to-day existence – newspapers, magazines, letters, telephone messages, invitations to parties (pages 56 and 57). But perhaps neither of these activities is as paradoxical as it seems. For in both, Warhol the 'real' person has disappeared: in the first, behind a commercialized image; in the second, behind the objects in his life.

Camouflage Self-Portrait
Andy Warhol, 1986

opposite
Self-portraits in drag
Andy Warhol, 1981/82

'I paint pictures of myself to … I guess, yeah, to remind myself that I'm still around.'
Andy Warhol

'Who wants the truth? That's what show-business is for – to prove that it's not what you are that counts, it's what you think you are.'
Andy Warhol

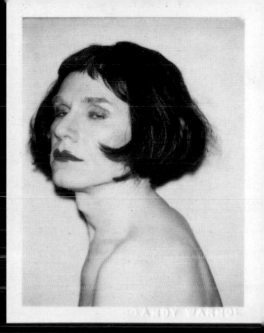

'No matter how good you are,
if you are not promoted right,
you won't be remembered.'
Andy Warhol

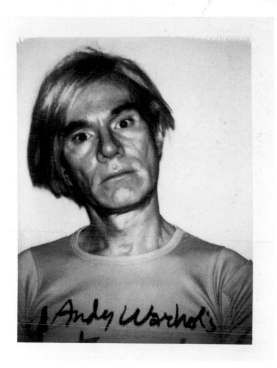

Self-portrait (in Interview T-Shirt)
Andy Warhol, 1977/78

below
Self-portrait (back, red T-Shirt)
Andy Warhol, 1977/78

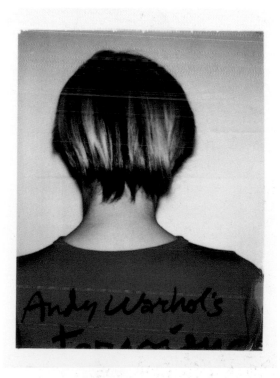

Inventory of Time Capsule 12
date of review: February 19, 1993
location: Crozier Fine Art Warehouse, New York City
present: Vincent Fremont (Estate), Matt Wrbican (Museum), Richard Hellinger (Museum)
time started: 10:15 am
time finished: 10:38 am
marks on box: top '[21]' 'T.C.' Ronnie Cutrone's handwriting
marks on box: sides '69-70' Ronnie Cutrone's handwriting

---

silver papered gift box, cont porcelain plate dec. with figure of a woman, approx 12" diam.

shipping tube, cont poster of sun image 'Love 1972' by Yves Saint Laurent

book, *a: a novel*, by AW, Kiepenheuer & Witsch, 1968, German edition, hardcover

mag., *After Dark*, Jan 1971

comic book, Marvel Comics, *My Love*, May 1970, 'Female Freedom'

mag., *Evergreen Review*, No. 85, Dec 1970

auction cat., Parke Bernet Galleries, NY, Dec 11-12 1970, *Americana: The Property of Channing Hare*, handwritten notes on back cover and throughout inside

mag., *Domus*, Sept 1970, Italian art and architecture

env., to AW, fr Heiner Friedrich, Dec 21 1970, in German

env., fr Evergreen, cont. 6 Polaroid photos of a man

env., to AW, fr Louis Waldon in Italy, Sept 2 1969

2 novelty miniature auto license plates, Texas 'BRD-SHT', 1970

newsp., *Park East*, Dec 31 1970, AW's film *Trash* mentioned on page 8

newsp., *Park East*, Jan 14 1971, AW's film *Trash* mentioned on page 8

auction cat., Parke-Bernet Galleries, *Art Nouveau & Art Deco*, Jan 28 1971, calculations on back cover

book, paperback, *Inside Creedence*, by John Hollowell, Bantam Books, 1971, inscr. 'for Andy Warhol /words fail me with you / much love / fr John Hallowell & Creedence / New York, 1971'

env., to AW, fr David Ryan of Minneapolis Inst. of Arts, re Art Deco exh at Cranbrook Academy, Nov 3 1970

mag., *Paris Review*, Fall 1970

2 typed sheets, suggestions re AW's film *Women in Revolt*, to AW, both signed 'To Andy from Jackie' [Curtis?]

large empty manila env., to AW Films Inc at 33 Union Sq W, fr Michael Findley of Richard Feigen Gallery

large empty manila env., labeled 'Andy-Bills & checks (General Business)'

large manila env., autograph request, fr John Buchanan of Markham Ontario, Jan 14 1970

book, hardcover, *Traditions of Japanese Art: Selections from the Collection of Kimiko & John Powers*, by John M. Rosenfield and Shujiro Shimada, Fogg Art Museum at Harvard University, 1970, inscr 'For our friend Andy Warhol with warm regards and

admiration. / Sincerely, / Kimiko Powers / John Powers / November 23, 1971' with Japanese lettering at sides

yellow plastic tape dispenser with green tape

small china plate, blue decoration, Shenango, signed on bottom [Olety?] Johnson

b&w contact sheet, 2 small images of a man in NYU t-shirt

2 canvas pouches, cont small annct: 'Ulysse Lacard 43/100' on one side; 'Cette Sphere Represente_1/4.55166 x 10^28 Du Volume Du L'Universe' on other side, gray plastic tube and solid red ball

newsp, *Changes*, Vol 2, Issue 15, Nov 15 1970

small card, 'Compliments of William N. Copley'

mag, *The Advocate*, Nov 11–24 1970

mag, *New York*, opened to pp 35–34, 'Now is the time to buy a co-op', by Peter Hellman, Jan 11 1971

art gallery price list, Jack Glenn Gallery, includes prices for AW's Soup Can Banner – Marilyn Monroe – single (not illustrated) and Marilyn Monroe – complete portfolio of 10 silkscreens – and *Flowers*

env., to AW, cont letter, fr Jim Benton of Dorchester London, Nov 25 1970, re interest in Mrs Richard Burton [Elizabeth Taylor] purchasing print of her portrait

art sale catalog, Jack Glenn Gallery Important Graphics, 1971

book, *a: a novel*, by AW, Kiepenheuer & Witsch, 1968, German edition, hardcover

polaroid photo backing

env, to AW, cont 3 b&w polaroids of female impersonator, letter fr Dana Carter re film work

env., to AW, fr Jane Forth in Paris, Nov 17 1970

gallery opening annct, Martin Cohen Fine & Applied Art 1860–1935

exh inv, 'The Drawing Society National Exhibition 1970', Jan 12 1971, Finch College Museum of Art NYC

inv, Soul Champagne Dinner Party, Jan 1 1971, fr The Judson Three (Faith Ringgold – Jan Hendricks and Jean Toche), NY – all funds go to the legal defense of The Judson Three

card, to The Factory 33 Union Sq, Christmas greetings fr Washington DC Chapter Fan Club, posted Dec 24 1970 Stockton CA

small env, fr Nancy G. Haigh of Berkeley CA, to AW, Feb 28 1969

env, posted Mar 3 1969, contains two sheets of graph paper with short messages to AW

env, to Geraldine Smith c/o AW Pro, on Franco Rossellini stationery, fr Paul Frederick Zabara of Brooklyn NY, Sept 17 1969, posted Rome Sept 25 1969

small, bent strip of 16mm filmstrip

End of TC 1

'Life and living influence me more than particular people.'

Andy Warhol

'I used to have the same lunch every day for twenty years, I guess, the same thing over and over again. Someone said my life has dominated my art – I like that idea.'

Andy Warhol

'The primary creation of Andy Warhol is Andy Warhol himself.'

Harold Rosenberg

Contents of Time Capsule 44
Andy Warhol, mainly 1950–1973

Jeff Koons has cultivated the idea of the artist as media image or brand perhaps more than any other artist since Andy Warhol. A large part of Koons's artistic life has been devoted to promoting himself as the perfect 'designer' product. In 1988, for example, he produced a series of advertisements that were published in four major arts magazines: *Artforum*, *Art in America*, *Arts* and *Flash Art*. For each one, he took up a different role: the smart school teacher, the boyish playboy, the king and the pig.

He developed the 'Jeff Koons' brand even further by turning his 1991 marriage to porn star Ilona Staller (alias La Cicciolina) into a highly publicized media event. Over the next few years, the intimate details of their life together were played out in public in various forms. In 1989, for instance, a poster advertising *Made in Heaven*, a soft-porn movie starring Staller and Koons, was posted on a billboard on Broadway. In 1990, stills from the film and a life-size sculpture of the couple making love were exhibited at the Venice Biennale. They were, of course, the star guests at this art event, causing a media frenzy.

Koons has carefully crafted his public image through all of his art works, interviews and appearances. He has deliberately designed his 'autobiography' to meet not only the desires and expectations that others project onto him – including Koons, the pig – but also his own vision of what a successful artist should be.

The New Jeff Koons
Jeff Koons, 1980

'An autobiography is only to be trusted when it reveals something disgraceful. A man who gives a good account of himself is probably lying, since any life when viewed from the inside is simply a series of defeats.'
George Orwell

JEFF KOONS

Dd Ee Ff Gg Hh Ii Jj Kk Ll Mm Nn Oo

EXPLOIT
THE
MASSES

MENTALITY

BANALITY
AS SAVIOUR

must

SONNABEND · NEW YORK · MAX HETZLER · KÖLN · DONALD YOUNG · CHICAGO

Art Magazine Ads *(Art in America)*
Jeff Koons, 1988–89

Art Magazine Ads *(Arts)*
Jeff Koons, 1988–89

'I was trying to deal with people's desires. Also I think it was presenting the idea of the chameleon – that if one emulates what one wants to be, one can become that.'
Jeff Koons

'I want to have an impact in people's lives. I want to communicate to as wide a mass as possible. And the way to communicate with the public right now is through TV and advertising.'
Jeff Koons

JEFF KOONS

SONNABEND • NEW YORK   MAX HETZLER • KOLN   DONALD YOUNG • CHICAGO

Art Magazine Ads
(Flash Art)
Jeff Koons, 1988–89

I love
Denitsa

I love Denitsa
RASSIM®, 1996

The point of departure for Krassimir Krastev is the problem of how to present himself as an artist in the post-Communist society of his native Bulgaria. Rejecting the romantic cliché of the 'authentic' artist – pale, anxious, dishevelled – he decided instead to cultivate an image more like that of the superstars and celebrities who are forever in the spotlight of public attention. He reinvented himself as RASSIM®, the

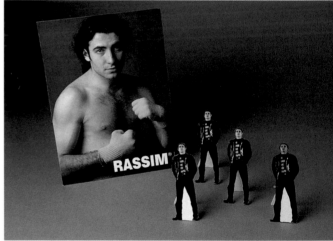

RASSIM®(installation view)
RASSIM®, 1996

'brand name' under which he now works. In his art, he uses the invented persona of RASSIM® as a means to explore the mechanisms and ideals of capitalist market forces, and he employs the forms and strategies of PR and mass-media publicity to do so. For instance, he filmed himself or had himself photographed with the accessories of modern living, such as cell phones and cigarettes, just as a star might endorse particular consumer products and lifestyles. These images, he says, exemplify the way that self-portraiture should now be done. RASSIM® is defined by the objects he possesses and surrounds himself with, so that any 'real' personality Krastev may have is masked or disappears. And, like Jeff Koons, he promoted his brand name by announcing his relationship with his girlfriend Denitsa through advertisements in art magazines.

Self-portrait with cigarette
RASSIM®, 1995

Self-portrait with GSM
RASSIM®, 1998

Corrections
RASSIM®, 1996–98

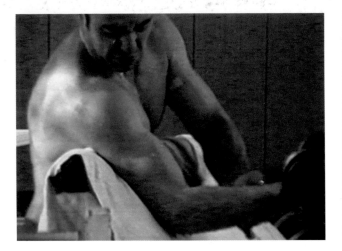

In another project, the video and poster work *Corrections*, RASSIM® 'sculpted' his body according to Hollywood standards. Over the course of a year and a half, he visited a gym every day and took special energy food and drinks, all in order to build the 'ideal' body. The whole process of transformation was documented and distributed in different forms – videos, posters, stickers, magazine ads – thus establishing RASSIM®'s image and lifestyle as an artistic trademark.

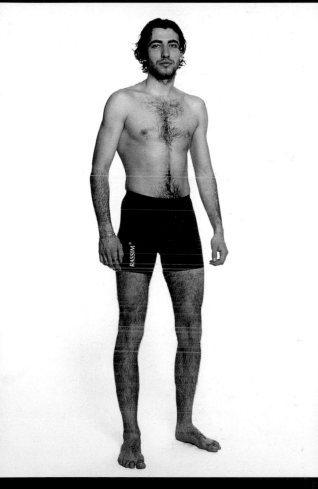

Corrections (Before)
RASSIM®, 1996

Corrections (After)
RASSIM®, 1998

In 1977, American artist Cindy Sherman began her series of *Untitled Film Stills*, in which she photographs herself in the pose of female movie characters. Rather than iconic stars, she selected scenes from lesser-known black-and-white films, especially B-movies, for she was most interested in exploring female stereotypes and cinema clichés.

In some of these images, traces of Sherman's technical apparatus (remote shutter release, for example) remain in view, deliberately left there by the artist to draw attention to the images' constructed nature. Being both photographer and subject allows Sherman to both watch and be watched. She not only conceals her own identity beneath that of the actress she 'plays', but she also denies those actresses theirs, for they disappear behind Sherman's own standardized features. Identity is constantly borrowed in this endless photographic role-playing, and any individual autobiography dissolves.

top
Untitled Film Still #4
Cindy Sherman, 1977

above
Untitled Film Still #21
Cindy Sherman, 1978

opposite
Untitled Film Still #37
Cindy Sherman, 1978

'It has nothing at all to do with me. I work with myself, that's my material somehow, but the finished photograph has something more to offer than reflections of my "personality".... My photos are certainly not self-portraits or representations of myself, though unfortunately people always keep saying they are.'
Cindy Sherman

In 1968 French artist Christian Boltanski started to reconstruct his childhood. However, as he could not or would not always recall certain things and events with any clarity (if at all), and did not have any photos (or pretended he did not have any photos), he bridged the gaps in the reconstruction by using 'foreign' material or by manufacturing scenes. The project – still ongoing – takes many forms: booklets, performances, objects and installations. In the performance *Les reconstitutions de sa jeunesse* (*The Reconstructions of his Childhood*), he acted out characteristic childish behaviour. After this, he reconstructed in plaster objects he had owned as a child and recorded lullabies he remembered from that time.

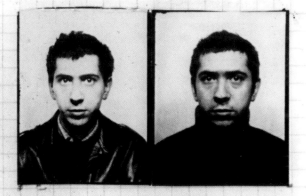

Christian Boltanski separated by five years and three months
Christian Boltanski, 1970

CHRISTIAN BOLTANSKI A 5 ANS 3 MOIS DE DISTANCE.

'Anyway I'm a rather constructed person,
and my reality is disappearing more and more.
I suppose it's partly like that for everyone, artist or not.
You decide what bit of yourself is to show or not.'
Christian Boltanski

'For various reasons I had major problems with my childhood, and so I invented one – or rather so many that I no longer have a childhood. I blotted it out by inventing a lot of fictional experiences. An artist plays with life – he no longer lives it.'

Christian Boltanski

Reconstruction of songs sung to Christian Boltanski between 1944 and 1946
Christian Boltanski, 1971

Comic Playlet
Christian Boltanski, 1974

In 1972, Boltanski published another two booklets, *10 Portraits photographiques de Christian Boltanski, 1946–1964* and *L'Album photographique de Christian Boltanski*. Both works purport to present the artist's authentic autobiography, but in fact they use various images that never show the same people twice, and none of them is Boltanski. The mixture of fact and fiction opens up an area of free play in which observers can tell their own stories and recall events from their own lives.

'There's no such thing as an autobiography. If you like Proust, it's because he does not speak so much about himself as about all of us – we have all been afraid of the dark and wished that our mother would say goodnight to us, and we've all been jealous, and we've all had a pretty daft great-aunt whom we were fond of…. The really interesting autobiographies are those that do not talk about the author, but about every reader.'
Christian Boltanski

ROOM THREE

FACTS

What is a better record of a life: a person's subjective memories or
the raw data of day-to-day existence? All of these artists seek to
accurately represent their experience of life, either by hiding behind a set
of verifiable facts or by mixing the emotional with the purely quantifiable.
But how much of a life can be documented at all?

Every year since 1966, On Kawara has produced between 30 and 241 so-called 'Date Paintings', each one showing nothing but the date on which it was made, written in the convention of the country in which it was executed. If Kawara does not finish the painting by midnight on the respective day, he destroys it. The process of painting takes many hours and demands high concentration from the artist. The paintings are then stored in individual boxes, onto which a clipping from that day's newspaper is glued. Kawara exhibits his 'Date Paintings' with books (such as *I met*, *I read*, *I went*), postcards sent to friends (*I got up at*) and telegrams (*I am still alive*). In this accompanying documentation, he delivers a detailed report of his life, but one that is limited to some of his daily recurrent acts and activities. He ignores any personal comments or anecdotes, thus confining himself to the bare essential facts of his day-to-day existence.

In June 2002, we received an e-mail from the British curator Jonathan Watkins, who had forwarded to Kawara our invitation to be in this book. It said, 'On Kawara does not want to be included in a book on autobiography.'

BS: At first I was quite sad about his rejection. How were we supposed to deal with it? Should we give up or should we try to contact him personally? But it's difficult to get hold of his personal details, like a telephone number or address.

JY: That fits with his general attitude. The only information available in published biographies of him is the number of days he had lived up to that point in time; no birthday, no place of birth, or any other personal hints. It therefore makes sense that he remains unapproachable, and almost invisible.

BS: I can't remember a single photograph of him!

JY: Could we include him without his approval?

BS: Do you mean show his work without his permission by approaching institutions that own it? We could, but we shouldn't.

JY: But it would be a pity to produce a book on 'autobiography' without including him.

BS: Well, that's obviously what he doesn't want: to be included. I guess the main reason is that he equates autobiography with strong involvement in subject matter. His use of registration and protocol systems contrasts completely with the subjectivity of autobiography.

JY: But we're not interested in the celebration of the subject anyway. In fact quite the opposite.

Links to On Kawara's work

Bibliography

On Kawara: 1973, Produktion eines Jahres – One Year's Production, edited by
Marianne Schmidt, Kasper König and Johannes Gachnang. Bern: Kunsthalle, 1974

On Kawara, text by Lucy R. Lippard. Los Angeles: Otis Art Institute, 1977

The Daily Images of Power: On Kawara from Day to Day, edited by Yvon Lambert.
Text by René Denizot. Paris: Yvon Lambert, 1979

On Kawara: I Am Still Alive. Berlin: Galerie René Block, 1979

On Kawara: Continuity/Discontinuity 1963–1979, edited by Björn Springfeldt.
Stockholm: Moderna Museet, 1980

Documenta 7, edited by Saskia Bos. Two volumes. Kassel: D + V Paul Dietrichs, 1982

On Kawara, texts by David Higginbotham, Jörg Johnen, Seigou Matsuoka and Anne
Rorimer. Dijon: Le Consortium, 1985

On Kawara: 1976–1986, Berlin, edited by René Block. Text by Wolfgang Max Faust.
Berlin: DAAD, 1987

On Kawara 1952–1956 Tokyo: History of an Odd Generation, by Makoto Oda.
Tokyo: Parco, 1991

On Kawara 1952–1956 Tokyo: At the Junction of Time and Space, by Tadashi
Yokoyama. Tokyo: Parco, 1991

On Kawara: Date Paintings in 89 Cities, edited by Karel Schampers. Texts by Teresa
O'Connor, Anne Rorimer and Karel Schampers. Rotterdam: Museum Boymans-van
Beuningen, 1991

On Kawara, edited by Jean-Christophe Ammann, Susanne Lange, Rolf Lauter and
Mario Kramer. Text by René Denizot. Frankfurt am Main: Museum für Moderne
Kunst, 1991

On Kawara, 1969. Reprint of the books *I Went, I Read, I Met, Journal*. Cologne:
König, 1992

On Kawara: Again and Against, edited by Kasper König, Ulrich Wilmes and Robert
Wilk. Text by Wolfgang Max Faust. Frankfurt am Main: Portikus, 1992

On Kawara: 1964 Paris – New York, Drawings, edited by Roland Wäspe. St Gallen:
Kunstverein, c. 1997

On Kawara: Horizontality, Verticality, edited by Ulrich Wilmes. Cologne: König, 2000

Internet

www.diacenter.org/exhibs/kawara
www.dnp.co.jp/museum/nmp/nmp_i/articles/kawara.html
www.artcyclopedia.com/artists/kawara_on.html
www.museenkoeln.de/ludwig/temp/0103_kawara
www.assemblylanguage.com/reviews/Kawara.html
1001.org/Artists/Kawara.html
www.portikus.de/ArchiveK0013.html
wwar.com/masters/k/kawara-on.html

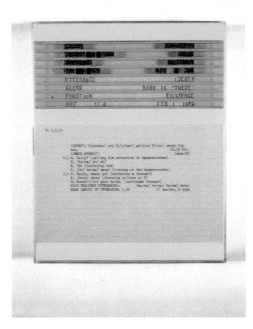

British artist Mary Kelly produced the *Post-Partum Document* between 1973 and 1979, following the birth of her son. It was a project grounded in the theoretical and political practice of the Women's Liberation movement of 1970s Britain. Consisting of seven sections – an introduction and *Documentations I–VI* – the piece takes the form of a detailed list of data derived from the lives of the artist and child. She reports not only on such matters as his daily food intake and defecation patterns, but also on her growing relationship with him, so that statistical information is presented alongside subjective feelings and observations. Baby vests, stained nappy liners, first utterances, markings, hand imprints, and so on, attest to the development of the child. Personal, subjective reflections are juxtaposed with more distanced, 'scientific' analysis and diagrams.

opposite and above

**Post-Partum Document 1973–79,
Documentation II, Analysed Utterance
and Related Speech Events**

Mary Kelly, 1975

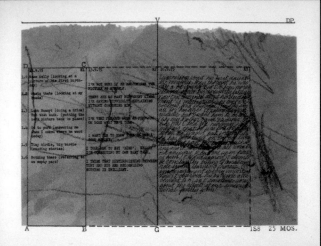

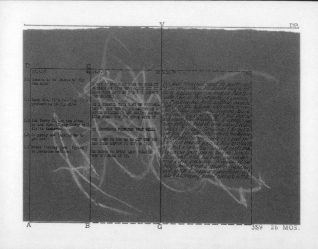

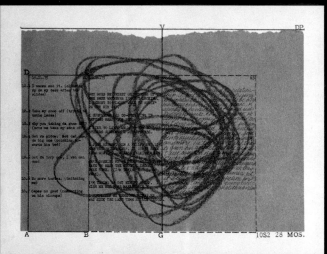

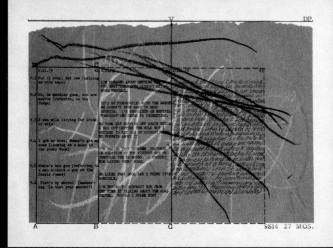

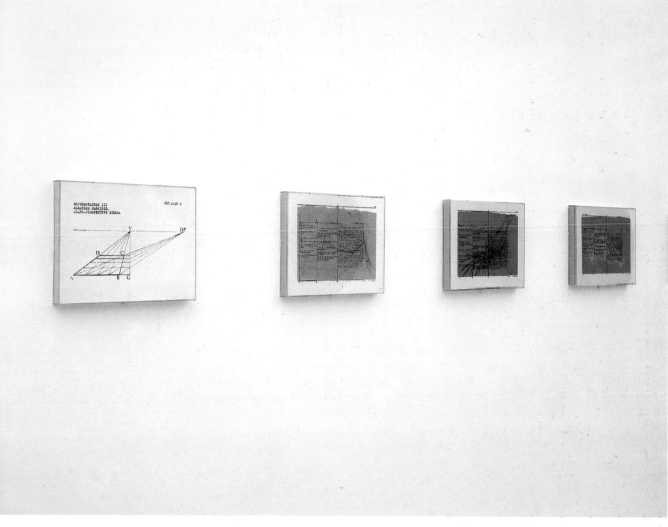

opposite and above

**Post-Partum Document 1973–79,
Documentation III, Analysed Markings
and Diary Perspective Schema**

Mary Kelly, 1975

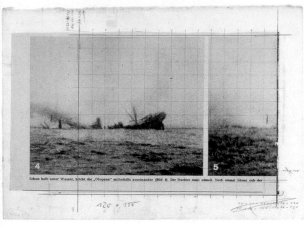

German painter Gerhard Richter began assembling his photograph archive *Atlas* in 1962. This now huge collection of images has become a unique record of contemporary history, documenting events of worldwide importance but from a personal point of view. In the beginning, it consisted mainly of amateur snapshots, clippings from magazines and newspapers, and anything else Richter thought was artistically or historically important or that interested him for any reason. Later on he began adding personal images, such as photographs of his friends and family. The personal picture – of his wife, or his child – comes to transcend the private sphere and instead stands for a generalized image of a mother and a child like those found in an array of representations

ranging from art-historical to the popular mother-child image found in newspapers and magazines. Richter's own autobiography is therefore told through *Atlas* but it merges with a huge transpersonal universe of factual images, where images of purely personal significance are interspersed with those of celebrities and historic events

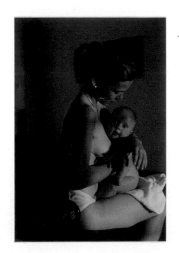

'Reminiscences, even extensive ones, do not always amount to an autobiography.... For autobiography has to do with time, with sequence and what makes up the continuous flow of life. Here, I am talking of a space, of moments and discontinuities.'

Walter Benjamin

AUTHENTICITY

Are artists who display the most intimate details of their lives for public scrutiny simply egomaniacs? How much do we, the audience, project ourselves onto their revelations? Do we see them as they really are ... or as we are?

At first glance, Austrian artist Elke Krystufek seems to champion the authenticity of personal expression. In her paintings, videos and performances, she appears to be offering the most private revelations about herself and her life, whether in the form of her own photo album, her expressive self-portraits, or her intimate poses and explicit actions. But no matter how 'private' or 'real' these public displays may seem, they turn out to be more or less stereotypical gestures, based on socially conventional roles and preconceived patterns of behaviour.

Krystufek repeatedly takes up different clichéd personae and poses in her work. She slips into white or black characters, shifts gender, is exotic, an innocent child, a grown-up woman, a pin-up, groupie or feminist. Her art presents itself as an authentic autobiography, but it has less to do with her own real life story than with how outside influences and ideas affect one's own identity and sense of self. Krystufek's self-presentations therefore question the very possibility of an authentic, direct expression of self, and continually point to their own derivativeness and artificiality.

Collector Krystufek with Ketty La Rocca
Elke Krystufek, 2002

'I think it is a crucial point that I have already been a public figure for ten years, and that happened very early. That means that I have no life history as an adult where I was not already a public figure. For this reason, my work can never be personal to that extent because I have never had this kind of personal life. It has actually always been a dialogue with the public.'
Elke Krystufek

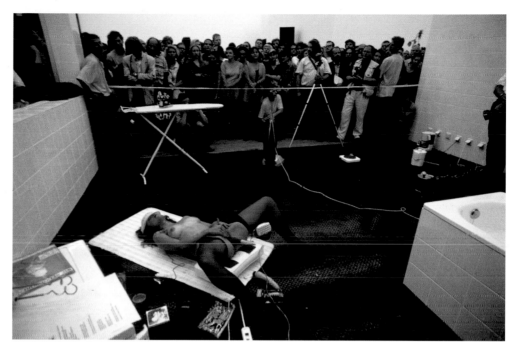

Satisfaction
Elke Krystufek, 1994

Performance for short-sighted people
Elke Krystufek, 2002

I speak painting
Elke Krystufek, 2002

'The art business has a great deal to do with projections ... as a person, you are confronted with this daily. A self-portrait is also an opportunity to correct that again and again.'

Elke Krystufek

opposite
Reminder (Exiter)
Elke Krystufek, 2001

Your Daddy
Elke Krystufek, 2001

Europe Works in Germany
Elke Krystufek, 2001

Krystufek began painting self-portraits in 1995 with a series in which her features merge with those of 1960s icon Edie Sedgwick, who was a model and leading light at Andy Warhol's Factory. In other portraits, Krystufek mingles her features with those of Marilyn Monroe and Vincent van Gogh. In later portraits, like the ones here, her references are less specific: she merely looks naïve, shy, fragile or aggressive. In each image, her expressive painting style suggests an intimate revelation of her character. But just behind this immediacy, this seemingly authentic depiction of self, are always the media clichés and stereotypes of our time – whether the 'famous film star', the 'tourist' or the 'perfect daughter' – so that ultimately Krystufek's self-portraits again question the very possibility of an autobiography that is authentic and unique to her alone.

British artist Tracey Emin is another who offers up the most intimate details of her personal life to her audience in an apparent show of authenticity. In *Everyone I Have Ever Slept With 1963–1995*, for instance, she announced all the people she had slept with – platonically or sexually. The list of 102 names sewn inside a tent included her grandmother, her aborted foetus, her friends and her lovers. Viewers were encouraged to peer inside in a voyeuristic way to discover the revelations – to peer, that is, into Emin's own private life. But we must take her at her word that she slept with all these people. We can never be sure that she is telling the truth.

Exorcism of the last painting I ever made
Tracey Emin, 1996

Exorcism of the last painting I ever made was the title of a performance that took place in the Cologne Kunstverein Gallery in 1995. Spatially separated from the viewer but still visible, Emin painted completely naked, only stopping to take several short breaks. When Emin was not on view, traces of personal use, of privacy and authenticity, could be seen. The paintings themselves partly show thoughts that crossed the artist's mind as she worked. They function as a 'painterly diary' and refer to her physical and psychological condition, such as 'The first cigarette of the day always makes me want to shit, this is the first; I love you Sarah'. Once again, Emin was presenting the intimacy and privacy of a 'private' space within a 'public' room, and her nakedness seemed to underline that privacy. But, in fact, since everything took place in public, the threshold of privacy had been crossed permanently or, to put it differently, 'privacy' was just quoted to attract people, to push them into a voyeuristic situation.

My Bed
Tracey Emin, 1998

When she was nominated for the prestigious Turner Prize in 1999, Emin decided to show her actual bed in the Tate Gallery in London. The installation included stained pillows, cigarette butts, empty vodka bottles, used tampons, tissues, dirty knickers, and so on. Once again, she seemed to be presenting the reality of her daily life just as it was, without any kind of mediation or

**Everyone I Have Ever Slept With
1963–1995**
Tracey Emin, 1995

editing of the facts. The intimate nature of the work provoked some strong reactions among visitors to the exhibition, including two Chinese performance artists who bounced up and down on the bed. And yet in both *My Bed* and in *Everyone I Have Ever Slept With*

1963–1995, while Emin certainly is making selected parts of her autobiography visible, it is the visitor who completes the work by projecting their own imagined ideas about her life and character, by speculating on what might have happened in the bed or in the tent.

French artist Sophie Calle mixes her own versions of her life with those provided by other people, or else she subjects herself to the image other people have of her, so that the borders between the authentic real and the imagined are constantly blurred. In this way, her autobiography – whether she invents part of it, submits her daily life to strict rules, or lets others describe her and her actions – functions as an interface, where different people's ideas and projections about her life meet.

In *Suite vénitienne*, Calle followed a stranger to Venice and then around the streets of the Italian city. Slipping into the role of a detective, she stuck hard on the heels of the observed and got emotionally more and more involved in the 'case'. In *The Shadow*, the tables were turned and she was herself followed, this time by a real detective employed by Calle's mother, at the artist's request, to track her movements around Paris for a whole day and to deliver a written report on her schedule; photographs were to underpin the report. Calle, who knew that the detective was watching her, wanted to attract him and led him around. Finally the roles were reversed: the watcher ended up being watched by Calle. In both cases, there is a precise list of the person's movements – drawn up by the artist and by the detective respectively – and a moment of intersection. Calle asks of the detective following her, 'Is he enjoying this wasted, diffuse and fleeting day that I've offered him – our day?', and concerning the stranger in Venice, she says, 'I mustn't forget that I have no feelings of love for Henri B.'

It remains open as to what constitutes 'real' life and what constitutes a performance staged for the benefit of the other or the camera. Photographs serve Calle as 'evidence' of the factuality and authenticity of events, as well as of her own existence, but they only 'prove' what is described by the accompanying text, while this in turn only describes what is shown in the photograph. In other words, photograph and text authenticate each other, but neither can in any way 'prove' anything factually.

'I followed strangers through the streets. Just for fun. One day, in January 1980, I followed a man and lost track of him a few minutes later. By chance he was introduced to me that same evening, and he told me about his forthcoming trip to Venice. I decided to follow him.'
Sophie Calle

Wednesday 13 February
11:00 I am wearing a beige mac, a scarf and sunglasses…
21:00 This evening is my first outing as a blonde…

Thursday 14 February
Midnight From the Accademia bridge I shout his name…

Saturday 16 February 1980
11:10 After three hours of constant coming and going,
I think I see him. I dash forward. It isn't him.

Tuesday 19 February
15:20 Right in the middle of Campo San Angelo I see him.
He turns his back to me and photographs a group of
children who are playing. Quickly I do the same…
I'm afraid he will suddenly whip round and see me
crouching in the filth. I decide to pass silently behind him
and to wait for him further on. I lower my head and scurry
across the bridge. Henri B. doesn't move. I could touch him.

Thursday 21 February
11:30 I give him one last chance: I count to a hundred,
he doesn't appear, I go.

Sunday 24 February 1980
10:08 HIM. The woman is following him.
They are both carrying bulky luggage…
10:10 I cease following Henri B.

opposite
**The Shadow
(installation view)**
Sophie Calle, 1981

this page
**Suite vénitienne
(details)**
Sophie Calle, 1980

'In April 1981, following my instructions, my mother went to the Duluc Detective Agency. She commissioned them to watch me and prepare a written report on how I spent my time, and to take a series of photos as evidence of my existence.'
Sophie Calle

'I'm a travelling painter. I paint images for board and lodging. The world wants to be seen! I travel to places where there are hosts for me.' Following the tradition of travelling craftsmen, German artist Antje Schiffers made a four-month trip to Russia, Kazakhstan and Kirghizia in 2002. Her artistic project included detailed preparations in advance of the trip, including learning the languages of the countries she was going to visit. Once there, she painted for her living, and documented, filmed and wrote about the whole experience. Like letters from far away, she sent these 'diaries' home as part of the project, and – in the case of the trip to Russia – they were published in a German newspaper while she was still travelling.

But Schiffers is not just a hiking artist but also an ambassador for her country. By organizing lectures, screenings and exhibitions back home in Germany, she in turn becomes a mediator for the countries, cultures and families she has come across. The documentation of her personal experiences provides a seemingly authentic record of her life that is far away from the conventional touristic and voyeuristic images brought back by ordinary holidaymakers. Even so, Schiffers recognizes that she has created this autobiography: however authentic it appears to be, it remains an account she has written. 'The trip is a story that I invent at the same time as it is a part of lived experiences. I'm going to report about something that I have experienced and will experience.'

'Autobiography is not the story of a life; it is the re-creation or the discovery of one. In writing of experience, we discover what it was, and in the writing create the pattern we seem to have lived. Simply put, autobiography is a reckoning.'
Carolyn G. Heilbrun

gone to the steppe (details)
Antje Schiffers, 2002

gone to the steppe (details)
Antje Schiffers, 2002

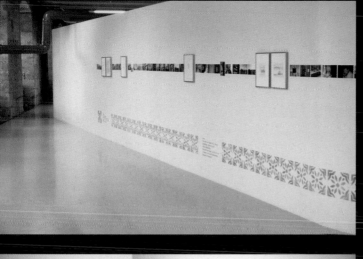

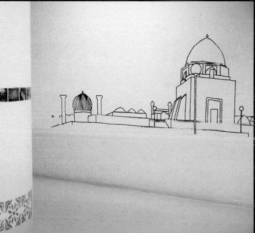

gone to the steppe (installation view)
Antje Schiffers, 2002

КИНОТЕАТР

Volksboutique Reference Library
Christine Hill, 2001

'*Volksboutique* is an entity incorporating everyday life and artistic practice.... It is about doing what you like and knowing what you want.'
Christine Hill

American Christine Hill conceived her *Volksboutique* enterprise in 1995. Meaning 'Boutique for the People', the project has since become the brand name under which she operates, as well as part of her own identity. The processes of production and organization are the subject of her art – the production of objects, of services and of art. From various 'mobile offices', she initiates different ventures, planning, organizing and distributing them in full view of the public. By showing the enterprise's workings in this way, she reveals the social structures underpinning everyday life. Hill describes the *Volksboutique* as 'an organizational venture … an exercise in labour, in public service, in conversational skill… Self Starter. Cottage Industry. DIY. Be your own boss!'

With *Volksboutique*, Hill enters an economic territory characterized by 'self-made' strategies in which questions of artistic self-management dominate. Having created several *Volksboutique* prototypes in various locations, in 1996 she opened a second-hand store in Berlin, where customers could buy moderately priced clothes according to their taste or after consulting the artist. She then established 'offices' in places that had played important roles in her life – Binghamton, New York, where she was born; Baltimore, where she studied; and Berlin, where she went after completing her studies. She now has her head office in Brooklyn, New York, where she lives. In each location, she designed and fitted out the complete workspace, making her own retro furniture and décor.

The location of the offices is not *Volksboutique*'s only link with Hill's autobiography, however. For the very project itself has become her entire life. The processes she displays are not the mere depiction or representation of her life, but actually *are* her life. We really see her at work, not playing at it. Hill says, '*Volksboutique* is not theatre. It is a production of life.' The result can seem bewildering. As one critic has put it, '*Volksboutique* straddles a line so fine that sceptical viewers seem about equally divided between those who can't believe it's art and those who can't believe it's life.'

top left
Volksboutique Prototype
Christine Hill, 1995

top right
Volksboutique Workspace
Christine Hill, 1996–97

above left
Tourguide Office
Christine Hill, 1999

above right
Pilot Production Office
Christine Hill, 2000

1229.
The more we do, the more we can do; the busier we are,
the more leisure we have.
William Hazlitt, excerpted from *Braude's Handbook of Stories*
for Toastmasters and Speakers, 1957

desk. n.
(defn).

1. a piece of furniture usually with a flat top for writing and
drawers or compartments. 2. a table, counter, or booth at
which specified, usually public services or functions are
performed: an information desk. 3. a lectern. 4. a department
of a large organization in charge of a specified operation:
a newspaper's city desk. 5. a music stand in an orchestra.

from *The American Heritage Dictionary*

© *Volksboutique* 2002

HYBRIDS

Those who stand between two or more cultures know better than anyone how one's identity, one's self-image and one's autobiography are constantly constructed and challenged by outside influences – the media, stories, films, snapshots and family lore. They, perhaps more than anyone, ask themselves, 'Who am I?'

Jun Yang was born in China in 1975 but left the country at the age of four to move to Austria with his parents. Having grown up in different cultural contexts, Yang examines the influence of mental and media images on his identity. His picture of China is based on vague memories, stories told by his parents, grandparents

and short sequences from mainly Hollywood movies set in Chinese restaurants. The rest of the time the screen remains black, while the artist's voice talks about his experiences. The Chinese restaurant has always played an important role in Yang's life, for it was the place in which he grew up. The installation for

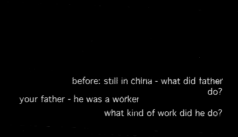

before: still in china - what did father
do?
your father - he was a worker
what kind of work did he do?

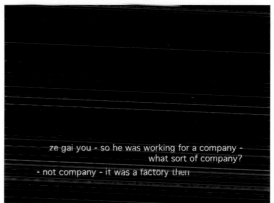

ze gai you - so he was working for a company -
what sort of company?
- not company - it was a factory then

coming home – daily structures of life – version D 00
Jun Yang, 2000

opposite
coming home – daily structures of life – version D 00
(installation view)
Jun Yang, 2001

'Whenever I watch my own videos I don't see "me"
personally – It feels like watching somebody else's story.'
Jun Yang

coming home – daily structures of life – version D 00
Jun Yang, 2000

'When my parents/our family moved to Europe, they ended up in Vienna – though they were planning to go to Belgium – Vienna was just a stopover place while waiting for the papers to be ready – to move on.... Once the papers were finally ready – they did not see a reason to move on – what difference did it make to them – Austria or Belgium – both were not China – both were empty – both without values – two countries without meaning – exchangeable – we stayed. I started to learn German instead of French and Flemish ... instead of going to the North Sea, I went skiing in the Alps – instead of mussels with french fries, "*moules frites*", I grew up with *wienerschnitzel*.'
Jun Yang

In 2001, Yang attempted to reconstruct the place of his birth in China. He used model-railway buildings, bridges, trains and pylons (for loudspeakers), which he had bought in Western Europe, where he grew up. Not surprisingly, Yang's town looks fragmented, for he could not remember every detail of a place he had left when he was only four years old. Interpretation therefore comes in: media images, stories, memories and experiences from his time in other cities overlap and produce a 'new' town. The title 'Arise! Arise! Arise!' is a reference to the title of the Chinese national anthem.

'It didn't feel like "my town" –
like the name of the place written
in my passport as a "place of birth".
It didn't feel like the place, the town –
people said so often in the last days
"you are ... European – but still you are ...
(like one would say like New Yorker,
or Berliner) you are one of us."'
Quote taken from ARISE! ARISE! ARISE!

Jun Yang

(2)

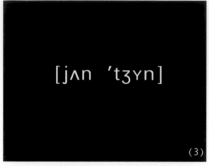

[jʌn ˈtʒʏn]

(3)

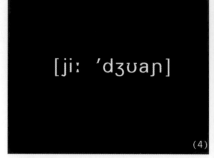

[jiː ˈdʒʊaɲ]

(4)

My name is (2) "Jun Yang"
"Jun" is the first name
"Yang" the family name...

...in chinese - in mandarin
chinese - it is pronounced (3)
- family name first...

...my parents on the other hand
are from a region with a
different dialect...
...they would say (4),.,

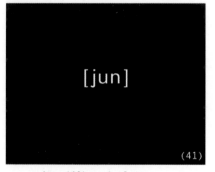

[jun]

(41)

[jʏn]

(42)

June Young

(43)

...Jun (41) was also
pronounced (42)...

...(42) which I thought sounded
more eloquent...

...or later June when I attended
to an english high school - which
is why I sometimes receive mail
for a certain Miss (43)...

Jun Yang and Soldier Woods also deals with Yang's
existence in and between two cultures, and the resulting
effect this had on his identity as he was growing up.
The video piece lists the different variations on his name
and its pronunciation given to him by his family, his school
teachers, his friends and others over the course of his life.

Jun Yang and Soldier Woods
Jun Yang, 2001

Re-Collection (Frankfurt Room)
Anny and Sibel Öztürk, 2000

Anny and Sibel Öztürk grew up in Germany but are of Turkish origin. In 2000 they constructed the *Frankfurt Room* – a typically Turkish room, containing various pieces of furniture, toys (some of which were actually their own), old photos and other documents, and a replica of their aunt's favourite divan, everything in a very 1970s style. The *Frankfurt Room* is based on a conglomeration of stories, memories and imaginings of one of the real rooms in which the pair grew up. Super 8 films of the two sisters as young girls are shown on a television screen. A series of colour drawings on the wall presents little black-haired Anny as a young child: 'I could talk when I was only six months old. What I loved doing most of all was to watch people and listen to them speaking,' is written under one picture from the 'Family Album' series.

Visualize (Dresden Room)
Anny and Sibel Öztürk, 2001

The *Dresden Room* was realized as a counterpart of the *Frankfurt Room*. In 2000, the Öztürks visited the former East Germany for the first time. They came across places that seemed perfectly compatible with the image they had in their mind of the East. Just as the two artists conceived of Turkey as a 'black-and-white' country because of the black-and-white photographs hanging in their grandparents' homes, they also believed that East Germany was a grey, bleak and faded country in which the sun never shone. Their perception of (life in) the East was ultimately the product of images they had seen as children in Czech or Polish movies. The *Dresden Room* contains furniture – an armchair, a sofa, a table and a sideboard – made of cardboard, fabric and self-adhesive imitation-wood-grain plastic veneer. Stills taken from famous DEFA movies (the Deutsche Film-Aktiengesell-schaft was the East German state's official film studio) hang on the walls. In both the *Frankfurt Room* and the *Dresden Room*, the Öztürks contrast their memories of a Turkish childhood with their views of childhood in East Germany, and in both cases they fall back on the clichéd images that underlie their view of the two cultures.

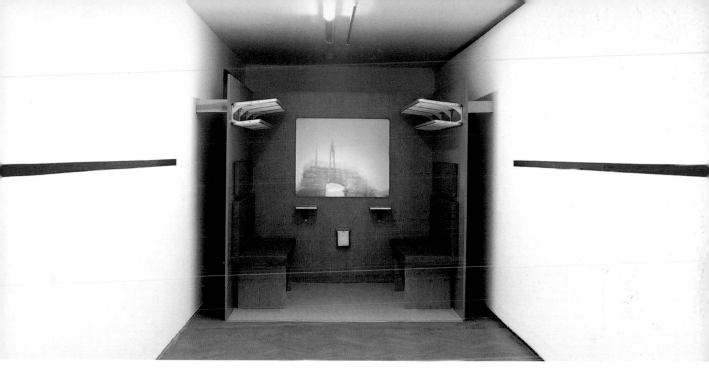

Preparations for a Journey
Anny and Sibel Öztürk, 2002

The installation *Preparations for a Journey* shows a
railway carriage in which one can travel back to the
Öztürks' childhood of the 1970s. In the window a Super
8 film plays, made by the artists' father in 1972, the year
of the family's emigration from Turkey. After watching
the film for a while, one cannot separate the family
scenes filmed at the Bosphorus from those filmed at
the Rhine. The recurrent sound reminds one at once
of a train and a film-projector. The reconstruction of
childhood reflects the Öztürks' diasporic experience:
images of Germany and Turkey intermingle constantly.

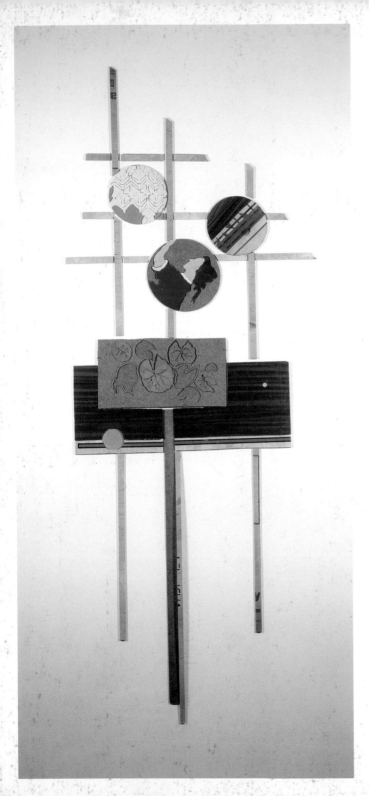

left and opposite
Neustädter News
TOBIAS Z. (in collaboration with Reinhardt,
Brigitte and Heide-Marie Tobias), 2001

The twin brothers Uwe and Gert Tobias were born and brought up in Neustadt, a village in Siebenbürgen, the German part of Romania, but both have lived in Germany since 1985. In 1999, they started to work under the label TOBIAS Z. ('Z.' stands for the German word *Zwillinge*, meaning 'twins'). Their family background forms the starting-point of their artistic work as they try to recollect their childhood in Romania.

In their mixed-media piece *Neustädter News*, TOBIAS Z. invited their parents and sister to express their relationship to Romania by creating a work using the media of their choice. Their father decided to reconstruct in plywood the objects the family brought with them when they moved to Germany; their mother embroidered a traditional motif from her native country and knitted a replica bell from the local church; while their sister decided to translate an old embroidered scene into a modern collage using international fashion magazines. The brothers, for their part, reconstructed their old village sign, which looks like an abstract piece of art (left). These objects were accompanied by interviews with the family members, in which they talk about their art works and their relationship to Romania. In summer 2000, TOBIAS Z. travelled back to Romania for the first time. They interviewed the local priest Klaus Daniel, whose perception of the Saxonian community is juxtaposed with memories of the Tobias family. In the work of TOBIAS Z., different perspectives on Siebenbürgen meet: the past and the present mix and can no longer be separated.

Reinhardt Tobias

'… When we were leaving and you packed the cases, how did you go about choosing the things you would take? We already had information from people who'd emigrated before us. The place and the beginning were uncertain. One took what one considered necessary for a new beginning…'

Brigitte Tobias

'… The motifs were gathered from one generation to another and then published as a collection. Of course the motifs varied from place to place. Then from the collection one could pick out motifs as required.…'

Heide-Marie Tobias

'… Everyone knew you. If you'd been dancing on the table, the next day the whole village knew about it. Above all they talked about it in the kitchen. Social control. Pretty awful, eh? Yes, that was the drawback.…'

Father Klaus Daniel

'… And now what's happened is that the young people have gone and the old have stayed.… I can't say that the new generation – children of mixed marriages or children from the Romanian population – who come for religious instruction in the Protestant faith show any sign of continuing our Siebenbürgen Saxon culture.…'

Rirkrit Tiravanija is a Thai artist born in Argentina who, after years in New York, now lives in Bangkok and Berlin. The interplay of cultural identities is a primary theme in his work, which usually takes the form of everyday social interactions re-staged within the space of a gallery or art institution.

Tiravanija's works are both essentially real and entirely constructed. One really can eat, drink, sleep, listen to music or converse in his spaces, which are conceived for specific venues. In the Cologne Kunstverein Gallery, for instance, he installed a replica of his own flat, complete with furniture, functioning bathroom, stocked fridge, etc. (opposite). The space was available day and night to anyone who wished to use it, whether to watch TV, have a bath, cook a meal or throw a party. In the Secession Building, Vienna, Tiravanija invited visitors into a miniature replica of the famous Los Angeles house by Modernist architect R. M. Schindler (left), a utopian architectural experiment designed to stimulate novel forms of social interaction. But these reconstructed spaces are not in themselves Tiravanija's art: as he himself says, his art consists of 'what happens between people', the social structures of daily life and human relationships.

Tiravanija constantly brings motifs from his own life into his works – his nomadic existence between numerous different cultures, for example, or his residence in New York. But these always occur side by side with references to media, aesthetic, social, cultural and institutional conventions. The result is that his own personal autobiography appears merely as a quote from time to time against a broader cultural background.

Untitled 2002 (Schindler)
Rirkrit Tiravanija, 2002

Untitled 1996 (tomorrow is another day)
Rirkrit Tiravanija, 1996

Untitled 1999 (caravan)
Rirkrit Tiravanija, 1999

ROOM SIX

RACE

Racial difference creates a wall of expectations that artists must
surmount before they can communicate anything of themselves.
The legacies of racism, for an individual as for a society, are anger,
frustration and pain. Such legacies can leave a deep mark on
ono'o identity and life. Autobiography can become the
story of dealing with discrimination and prejudice.

'I actually want to change people, I want my work to help people stop being racist whether they ask for it or not. Just as movies and encounter groups can change people, so, maybe, can my art.'

Adrian Piper

In an article written in 1992, 'Passing for white, passing for black', the American artist and philosopher Adrian Piper described the (her) problem of being a white-skinned member of a black family, someone who does not fit into existing categories of race. Several years earlier, she had dealt with a similar subject: in her photo and text installation *A Tale of Avarice and Poverty*, she told the fictive story of her father's family, a story full of romanticism and psychopathology that mixes traces of the artist's own autobiography with imagination in a tale about racism within a single family and a character's denial of her own identity and heritage.

A TALE OF AVARICE AND POVERTY

Once, long ago, there was a woman who was very beautiful, intelligent, and strong-willed. She was one of five sisters, all beautiful, intelligent and strong-willed, all competing with one another, all school teachers before they married.

Her father was a minister, a tall, handsome, charismatic man who later lost his faith and became a lawyer. Her mother was a local beauty, temperamental and imperious. The woman's family was a very important one where they lived, and very proud and well to do. They were not quite white. But they were all very fair-skinned, pale and pink with visible blue veins in their hands and wrists, amber eyes and wavy auburn hair. They disdained their darker-skinned brethren, whom they referred to as "niggers" and "pickaninnies". Whites, they contemptuously called "crackers".

The woman was too beautiful and strong-willed, domineering, really, to marry happily. Her first husband, a rich and handsome lawyer like her father, was a scoundrel and philanderer. He left her with two young sons, to journey to another part of the country, where he started another family and passed for white. The woman knew that he hoped thereby to recover his share of his family's aircraft company, from which he had been disinherited. Her second husband, an equally rich and handsome surgeon and her dead sister's widower, died young, of a heart attack, and left her with a small daughter and an unrevised will.

The woman was also too strong-willed, domineering, really, to be a good mother. Her eldest son wanted to be an historian, or perhaps a Jesuit priest. But she insisted that he become a lawyer, so he could help her recover her second husband's estate from her dead sister's family. She was always admonishing her children to keep their good fortune to themselves, lest the spiteful and envious try to deprive them of it. Her younger son wanted to be an artist, and drew beautifully. But she insisted that he become a doctor, so he could take care of her in old age.

Her younger son tried to satisfy her, and failed. He was admitted to dental school, at least, hated it, dropped out, and worked for the post office for the rest of his life. He was a shy and gentle man, retiring and vulnerable, and very kind.

Her elder son tried to satisfy her, harder, perhaps, because his father and grandfathers had been lawyers. Or perhaps it was because she wept and implored him and tried to instill in him her own wrath and righteous indignation at her dead sister's family. But he, too, ultimately failed. He became a real estate lawyer, hated it, and, after her many phone calls, drank deeply and often. He retired early to become a hospital administrator. He, too, was shy and gentle and sardonic, Jesuitically philosophical, radical in his thinking, and quietly stubborn. Once the woman used the word "nigger" in the presence of his family, and he forcibly put her out of the house. He made no serious effort to recover his stepfather's inheritance.

Only with her youngest child, her daughter, did the woman seem to have any success. She was determined that her daughter would vindicate her, would make something of herself that no one, no matter how spiteful or envious, could ever take away. She brought up her daughter very carefully, and rewarded her for working hard at school. The girl was shy and pretty, and stammered slightly. The woman insisted that her eldest son and his fiancée chaperone her on dates, and that she be home by ten o'clock. Her son ignored these strictures, and allowed her privacy and freedom. As her daughter got older, the woman began to fear that even her sons and their families might have a bad influence on her, and separated her from them as much as possible.

At sixteen, the woman's daughter was the first negro woman to attend the best of the seven sisters colleges, and later the first to attend the best of the ivy league medical schools. She became a child psychiatrist, married another, and moved with her family to a distant part of the country. The woman, her two sons, and the rest of their families were all very proud and somewhat in awe of her, though they heard less and less from her as the years went by, and then, after some requests from her for family mementos, nothing at all.

As the woman grew older, her obsession with recovering her second husband's estate grew more pronounced, and her phone calls, tearful and confused, to her eldest son more frequent. At this time he was still practising law, impractically: working part time in the ghetto and part time in the financial district, being paid with cakes, mended shirts, and auto repairs by his insolvent clients. He drank more and more heavily. His wife grew bitter. Concerned not to spoil his only child, whom he treasured, he withdrew from her as she entered adolescence. She became increasingly rebellious and unhappy, took drugs, ran with street gangs, was jailed and institutionalized, and left home to become a dancer (in later life she took a perverse and macho pride in her ability to look hard facts squarely in the face). Finally his wife asked him to leave. He went to live with his mother, who was by then very sick, hysterical, and unable to care for herself. In her apartment she grew thinner, weaker and more and more unsteady and ashamed. It seemed not unlikely that they would die together, the mother of resentment and venality, the son of malnutrition and despair.

Suddenly the woman's daughter appeared from across the country, and, ignoring her brother, without telling anyone, took her mother back home with her. Later, from across the country, she called her brother's wife to apologize, explaining that she had thought it best to let her brother hit bottom, alone, so that he could pull himself back up. By that time, his wife had gotten him into a hospital where he gradually recovered. Together they found their daughter and brought her home, where her tactlessness cleared the air and drew them close once more. He stopped drinking, returned to his family, and never practised law again. The woman died peacefully, in her daughter's care, having never ceased to ask about her sons, their families, her inheritance, and her many lawsuits.

After her death, many things changed for her children. Her eldest son was newly in love, again with his wife, who gossiped and joked affectionately with him, tolerated his smoking, and was tactful on the subject of his law practice. He was newly proud, again, of his daughter, who became a successful artist (for her uncle), academic philosopher (for her father), and wife (for her mother). She decided not to become a mother because (being free to do that for herself) she found she felt no need to do it at all. Her father counselled her to keep a low profile, lest the envious try to deprive her of success.

The woman's younger son continued to work at the post office, and often entertained his family with his beautiful drawings and paintings. His children were handsome, meditative, and intelligent. His eldest, a son, became a freelance computer programmer, and inherited his uncle's quiet sardonic wit. He married a calm, strikingly beautiful woman, and they worried together about spoiling their two lovely children. His second, a daughter, became a Muslim, nurse, and teacher, and bore a daughter and a son whose large black eyes, long lashes and winning smiles reminded everyone of their grandfather. His third child, a contemplative and darkly handsome son, became an artist and then a Muslim. His youngest son, a blond, blue-eyed charmer, went into the world to seek his fortune.

Providence seemed to smile on the woman's daughter. Her psychiatric practice went smoothly, and she had two happy and well-adjusted children, a son who became a lawyer and a daughter who became a doctor. Her husband became the president of a very large and powerful corporation, internationally known for its humanistic concerns. He negotiated successfully the release of American students held as hostages in a hostile third-world country, brought together scientists from the warring superpowers to collaborate on research for peace, and funded many young advanced scholars in the arts and humanities – including, unbeknownst to him, his own niece, whom he had never met.

For in the years following the woman's death, all was not well with her daughter at all. When her nephews wrote to tell her that the younger of her two brothers was gravely and tragically ill, she did not answer. When she returned with her family to that part of the country where she'd been born, her elder brother's wife wrote her but got no reply. Her brothers and their families read of her husband's success in the newspaper. When she was notified that the younger of her two brothers had finally and painfully died, she neither appeared at the funeral nor sent condolences. When they tried to telephone her, she did not return their calls.

It was after this that the woman's eldest son celebrated his daughter's marriage to a man who resembled him closely in sensibility. The daughter's husband, a psychologist, had occasion to collaborate with her aunt's former colleague. When, upon discovering the coincidence, the daughter wrote to her aunt to tell her, she, too, received no reply. Puzzled and hurt, she asked her parents to explain her aunt's silence. Together they speculated: Perhaps she never received the messages? Perhaps she was too ill to answer them? Perhaps, unwittingly, they had done something to her so vile and monstrous that she couldn't forgive them? Perhaps, having married a white man, she was passing for white? Or had decided to raise her children as white? Perhaps, having achieved status and financial security through her husband's success, she was afraid her relatives would ask her for favours? Or loans? Or to be invited to her dinner parties? Perhaps she feared that they would corrupt their children? Or were not rich enough to associate with them?

The more they speculated, the more dispirited and incredulous they became, and the more their pride in her accomplishments began to fade. Even to think about her became distasteful. This was particularly painful for the daughter, for whom her aunt had been an inspiration and role model. It occurred to the daughter that perhaps it was her aunt's achievements themselves that had crippled her character, and that this was the price of success. Being ambitious herself, the daughter quickly suppressed this thought.

Much later, she remembered her grandmother's admonitions about the spiteful and envious, and her competitive wars with her sisters for men, money and attention. She wondered whether her grandmother could possibly have meant to warn her own children's children, about another. The idea seemed absurd, bizarre.

Then the woman's eldest son became terminally ill, and was hospitalized. He asked to see his sister once more before he died. The last time had been in the squalor of her mother's apartment, almost twenty years before. Frantically, his daughter tried to reach her aunt, to no avail. She called her aunt's son, who did not return the call. She called her aunt's husband, who expressed sympathy, promised to convey the message, and referred her to another number which at that time, unluckily, was out of order. He did not identify himself to her as an uncle. The daughter wrote to inform her aunt of her father's impending death, but received no reply. Months later, her father died, without ever having mentioned his sister's name again.

His daughter was stricken by her aunt's silence. She thought about the pride and consolation her father had taken in his family, in being a part of it, and identifying himself with its history and the achievements of its members. The magnitude of the cruelty involved in knowingly depriving him of that consolation in the last, terrible moments before death took her breath away. She tried to imagine what it must be like to hate that coldly, to want to disown one's family, entirely, absolutely, and for ever, and found that she could not. Thus she discovered that her powers of imagination and hatred were limited.

After her father's death, the daughter decided to try once more to reach her aunt.

She called the number her uncle had given her, hoping that this time it would not be out of order. Her aunt answered the phone and said 'child psychiatry?'

The daughter answered, 'Dr._____, this is your niece_____.'

'Yes.' She replied.

The daughter continued, 'I'm calling to inform you that your brother _____ ...'

'Yes?' she interrupted.

The daughter went on, '... died yesterday morning of cancer, and that there will be a ...' The daughter struggled for control.

'... there will be a funeral mass for him on _____ at _____.'

'Thank you for calling,' she said.

'Goodbye', the daughter answered, and hung up.

Then she called each of her aunt's children, and left messages about the funeral mass on their answering machines.

At the funeral mass, many were wondering whether the dead man's sister would appear. His wife and daughter, grief-stricken and stung by her hardness, doubted it. But midway through the service, a small, pale young woman tiptoed into the church. She had a profile her relatives recognized from the newspaper photographs of her father. Her gaze swept the faces – tan, brown, black, white – of the congregation, before she sat down, alone, blushing, in an isolated corner pew. The object of intense scrutiny from the dead man's family and friends, she kept her face averted, and tiptoed out before the service came to an end. Afterwards, the dead man's daughter attended the same university at the same time, but received no reply

The grandmother of these young women, the beautiful and domineering woman with whom this story began, had done her best to be a good mother, in the face of what was for her an unjust and enforced deprivation. But she stifled her sons and crippled her daughter. She stifled her sons early on with her envy and vindictiveness, and they did not achieve a measure of freedom and tranquility until after her death. Her daughter she obsessively nurtured early on, with a mixture of jealousy and rancour, and the fruit of her labour did not reveal its deformity until after her death.

Her sons did their best to be good fathers, in the face of an overwhelming need for peace and privacy. They left the child-rearing to their wives, who nurtured, stunted, cajoled, threatened, loved, and bullied their children into adulthood, and raised them to regard their gentle, distant fathers with a mixture of pride and perplexity.

The woman's daughter did her very best, her professionally trained best to be a good mother, in the face of the yawning deprivation her mother had bequeathed her. And so, seeing her children through the eyes of the spiteful and envious, she deprived them, in turn, of their kinship, to protect them. For without their family, there would be no one to deprive their children of their good fortune.

Adrian Piper, 1985

Many clichéd images of Iran circulate: women covered with veils and oppressed by male society, religious fanatics who threaten Western values, a traditional nation stuck in the medieval past. Shirana Shahbazi

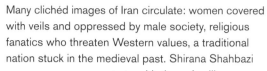

starts with these familiar categories, but then shows that the reality of life as an Iranian is far removed from the clichés. At first glance, her photographs seem to confirm the stereotypes of women in Iran wearing long coats and covering their heads. Yet they are depicted in situations that contradict the image of women confined to the home by the Islamic Republic: these women smoke in hotel lobbies, they work in offices and wander through modern leisure parks with their families. Shahbazi shows children wearing jeans and sneakers, surrounded by modern buildings and well-tended parks. She is interested in the ideas and prejudices that are attached to certain images, and in manipulated modes of perception. Modernity and tradition, Oriental and Western elements – these are simultaneously present in her photographs, with the result that it is impossible to arrive at a definitive interpretation and judgment of what life in contemporary Iran is really like for women like Shahbazi.

[Tehran-11-1998]
from 'Goftare Nik/Good Words'
Shirana Shahbazi, 2000–2

opposite
[Shahrzad-04-2002]
from 'Goftare Nik/Good Words'
Shirana Shahbazi, 2000–2

[Mard-03-2000]
from 'Goftare Nik/Good Words'
Shirana Shahbazi, 2000–2

opposite
[Manzareh-06-2002]
from 'Goftare Nik/Good Words'
Shirana Shahbazi, 2000–2·

**Goftare Nik/Good Words
(installation view)**
Shirana Shahbazi, 2001

opposite
**[Heyvan-01-2002]
from 'Goftare Nik/Good Words'**
Shirana Shahbazi, 2000–2

In South African artist William Kentridge's work, autobiographical elements, politics and social commentary intersect. *Johannesburg, Second Greatest City after Paris* is the first in a series of short animated films that revolve around the characters of Johannesburg property developer Soho Eckstein, a symbol of capitalist and colonialist corruption who bears a resemblance to Kentridge's grandfather, and the dreamer Felix Teitlebaum, who resembles the artist himself. Kentridge uses a simple animation technique for the film: some twenty-five drawings in charcoal and pastel on paper, which were constantly redrawn, were shot on 16mm film at each of the many stages of their evolution. Like captions in a silent movie, words appear on the screen, giving viewers information about the characters' emotions or the ongoing events. Set in the urban wastelands of Johannesburg and its surroundings, the film consists of two parallel stories: the founding and building of a mining town through the progressive growth of Eckstein's power, and the love affair between Felix and Soho's neglected wife, Mrs Eckstein. She is associated, in Felix's erotic fantasies, with water and bathing. This wet imagery of love and sex stands in opposition to the dry mining landscape, one of many binary conflicts between Felix and Soho. The film ends after a symbolic battle between the two male characters, who seem almost to become symbiotic parts of a single personality.

above and opposite
Johannesburg, Second Greatest City after Paris
William Kentridge, 1989

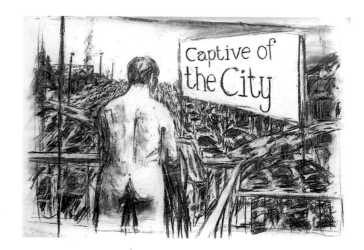

'My grandfather, Morris Kentridge, became a lawyer and a parliamentarian for the Labour Party. He was imprisoned as a socialist in the 1920s. He stayed a parliamentarian for Troyville, a suburb of Johannesburg, until the 1950s when he died. His wife, May Shaffner, my father's mother, was the daughter of a locksmith. Morris is interesting because in some way he becomes a model for Soho Eckstein. There is an early linocut, which I made in the '70s, based on a family photograph on the beach, where Morris Kentridge is sitting in a deck chair in his pin-striped suit. And of course, that only makes Soho a displaced self-portrait: there is a strong male family resemblance down the generations. There is even one moment in *Johannesburg, Second Greatest City after Paris* where he looks like my maternal grandfather.'
William Kentridge

The work of another South African artist, Tracey Rose, is inextricably tied up with her experiences of growing up in South Africa as a 'coloured person', the apartheid system's designation for someone of mixed race. Rose's art draws upon this autobiographical material, along with her Catholic upbringing and her German and Khoisan ancestry. The piece *Ciao Bella* consists of a collection of photographs and video projections in which Rose plays twelve different female characters who either fit stereotypes attributed to coloured people or adopt roles normally reserved for whites. The former group includes a tweed-clad 'Mami', a woman who beats herself with boxing gloves bearing the words 'Love me' and 'Fuck me', and Saartje Baartman, the Khoisan woman who was paraded naked before paying spectators in nineteenth-century London and Paris as the 'Hottentot Venus'; the latter group features Lolita, porn star La Cicciolina, and a gun-toting Bunnie girl. With burlesque gusto, Rose explores painful questions about identity, race, gender, sexual violence and politics that touch on her own life and that of her country.

top
Ciao Bella: Ms Cast Series 'Bunnie'
Tracey Rose, 2002

**Ciao Bella: Ms Cast Series
'Venus Baartman'**
Tracey Rose, 2002

top
Ciao Bella: Ms Cast Series 'Cicciolina'
Tracey Rose, 2001

Ciao Bella: Ms Cast Series 'Mami'
Tracey Rose, 2001

top
Ciao Bella: Ms Cast Series 'Lovemefuckme'
Tracey Rose, 2001

Ciao Bella: Ms Cast Series 'MAQEII'
Tracey Rose, 2002

top
Ciao Bella: Ms Cast Series 'Lolita'
Tracey Rose, 2001

Ciao Bella: Ms Cast Series 'Silhouetta'
Tracey Rose, 2002

top
Ciao Bella: Ms Cast Series 'Regina Coeli'
Tracey Rose, 2002

Ciao Bella: Ms Cast Series 'San Pedro'
Tracey Rose, 2002

POLITICAL SYSTEMS

No human life is untouched by a political system.
Many lives are marred by political upheaval or repression.
Even in times of peace, real change is painfully slow
and memories live on. Past injustices haunt present lives

Russian artist Ilya Kabakov is usually present within his installations, either in person or indirectly through photographs, autobiographical texts or personal belongings. One of his favourite materials is the rubbish that has accumulated in his studio over the years, and he used this in a series of installations beginning in the early 1980s. For him, the rubbish had both personal and social significance. It was not only expressive of his own psychological make-up, but it also provoked the 'special sensation, physical and mental, that everything which surrounded us living in the Soviet Union represented an enormous littered space'. In his installations, which have a powerful escapist theme, Kabakov linked the dirt and rubbish in his studio with the dirt and rubbish on the streets and in the everyday life of the Soviet Union – a link, that is, between his own autobiography and the political system into which he was born.

'An experiment of exhibiting my biography is the main theme running through a few installations. I am always looking back, into the past, and as a rule all of this has a depressing, sad quality. But when it concerns someone "else", then everything is just the opposite: the past begins to shine from the depths, similar to a radiant painting of paradise, sparkling and pure.'
Ilya Kabakov

10 Characters:
The Short Man (The Bookbinder)
Ilya Kabakov, 1988

10 Characters:
The Man Who Never Threw Anything Away
Ilya Kabakov, 1988

top left and right
10 Characters
Ilya Kabakov, 1988

Ilya Kabakov's installation *10 Characters* consisted of
ten windowless rooms and two corridors between them.
The structure followed the design of the communal
apartment common in the former Soviet Union, which
has one kitchen, one toilet and one bathroom for all
residents. The ceiling and the upper part of the walls
were painted in grey; the lower part and the floor, in
brown; some parts were covered with wallpaper; the
corridor and the rooms were illuminated by small hanging
lightbulbs. Apart from the 'The Man Who Flew into
Space from his Apartment', the rooms were almost dark.
In each, there was a series of objects which belonged
to the person who was supposed to live inside. Texts
offered background information on each 'resident':

The man who flew into his pictures
The man who collects the opinions of others
The man who flew into space from his apartment
The untalented artist
The short man
The composer
The collector
The man who describes his life through personages
The man who saves Nicolai Victorovich
The man who never threw anything away

Despite a depressive atmosphere, the rooms revealed
their occupants' desire to abandon the depression.
Each of them had invented their own special means
of departure, or way of ignoring their immediate political
surroundings, whether that be a collection of postcards,
a return to the past, the examination of rubbish, or a
flight into a picture or into space.

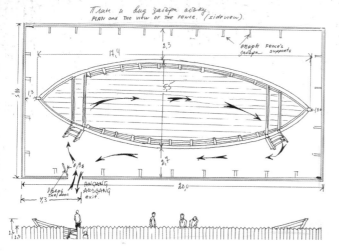

top left and right
The Boat of My Life (construction plans from above and side)
Ilya Kabakov, 1993 (left) and 1995 (right)

above left and right
The Boat of My Life
Ilya Kabakov, 1993

In *The Boat of My Life*, Kabakov presented the story of his life – his autobiography. It consisted of a wooden boat with stairways at each end. On deck there were twenty-five large cardboard boxes, filled with all kinds of household junk – shirts, coats, shoes, children's toys.

On top of each box lay a piece of cardboard on which photos, small objects and texts were glued. The texts were fragmented recollections of episodes in Kabakov's life. Each box represented its own period of his life. The last box was empty.

references to contemporary history, art and design, popular and consumerist culture, and personal biography, all influenced by his own processes of forgetting and remembering. The selection of images shown here, made especially for this book, includes a photograph of Wohnseifer as a child holding a model of Concorde in his hands; a photo of the Beach Boys singer Dennis Wilson, starring in the movie *Two Lane Black Top* (1971); stills from Wohnseifer's own road-movie *Freeway Race*; a collage showing the German painter Blinky Palermo with Elga Andersen, the principal actress in the film *Le Mans* (1970); and some snapshots from the opening of his first exhibition in Cologne in 1995. *Two Lane Black Top* and *Le Mans* gained cult status in the 1970s, and they are still among Wohnseifer's favourite movies. In these works, he is trying to trace both a personal and collective history. He attempts to present, through fragments of his own autobiography, the experience of growing up in the specific political and cultural conditions of 1970s West Germany.

THE BEST THING ABOUT TODAY

is THE IDEA OF TOMORROW

10-17-71
Johannes Wohnseifer, 2002

overleaf
Freeway Race
Johannes Wohnseifer, 2001

Untitled
Johannes Wohnseifer, 2002

opposite
Almost Abstract Study
Johannes Wohnseifer, 2002

1

09-15-95
Johannes Wohnseifer, 2002

'So what was I doing in this brief
memoir?... To tell the truth ...
I wasn't writing fiction.
I was writing memoir – or was trying to.
My desire was to be accurate....
Yet I am forced to admit that memory
is not a warehouse of finished stories,
not a gallery of framed pictures.
I must admit that I invented.'

Patricia Hampl

'When I was younger I could
remember anything, whether
it happened or not; but my
faculties are decaying now
and soon I shall be so I cannot
remember anything but the latter.'
Mark Twain

'A man's memory is bound to be a
distortion of his past in accordance
with his present interests, and
the most faithful autobiography
is likely to mirror less what a man
was than what he has become.'
Fawn M. Brodie

Autobiography and society are bound together in the work of Austrian artist Johanna Kandl. Paintings such as *Fritzelack*, *Visiting Mega-bauMax* and *Visit to the Studio* are linked not only to the general experience of living in Austria but also to Kandl's own specific life. Her parents once owned a small paint shop in Floridsdorf, a workers' district in Vienna, where the logo of the O. Fritze company appeared on the awnings. 'Fritzelack' (Fritze varnish paint) was one of the best-known trademarks in postwar Austria, and the idea of the clumsy apprentice who trips and spills the paint soon entered daily language. Even today, 'einen Fritzelack reissen' still has the meaning of falling, failing and being clumsy. The company's products have long disappeared, but 'Fritzelack' remains iconic in Austria.

From the late 1960s, superstores and large DIY centres dominated the marketplace, and small paint shops such as the Kandls' were doomed to decline. Karl-Heinz Essl is the owner of one of the biggest DIY centres in Austria, Mega-bauMax. He is also an important collector of contemporary art and owns several works by Kandl. The paintings she made for him deal with the dilemma she faced when working on the commission: they show the ironic relationship between Kandl and Essl, who stands for the big business that ruined her parents' livelihood but now supports her own. In these works, the personal details of her family life collide with more general comments on the political context in which she lives and the economic shifts within modern Austrian society.

SUCCESS IS HOW HIGH YOU CAN BOUNCE WHEN YOU HIT BOTTOM

opposite, above
Visiting Mega-bauMax
Johanna Kandl, 2002

opposite, below
Visit to the Studio
Johanna Kandl, 2002

below
Fritzelack
Johanna Kandl, 2002

Die Betriebsbesichtigung
Im Mega-bauMax in Wien-Stadlau, am 3. September 1997, um ca. 6h abends.

Das Ehepaar Essl bei uns im Atelier
Ein Sonntag im Februar 1997, ungefähr um 5 Uhr nachmittags
Gabi Bosch fotografiert.

'I'm fundamentally interested not only in art but also in social systems.
I never travel to other countries for the sake of art. Art for me is always a part
of the total social structure of a country, and sometimes it can help explain and
uncover that structure. Art is important to me only as a reflection of society,
not as a system that is concerned only with itself.'

Der Eingang zur Baustelle Mamulino
in Twer bei Moskau.
Wir fahren am Eingang zur Baustelle vor
Hier in Twer baut die Firma Maculan
Quartiere für russische Soldaten.
Viele Arbeiter kommen aus Korea.
Ein ungewöhnlich schöner und warmer F
Der Boden friert nur nachts
tagsüber scheint die Sonne und es taut.

im Februar 1995

In 1994, Kandl began work on a project about the withdrawal of troops from the Soviet garrison at Wünsdorf in the former East Germany and their resettlement in the areas north and north-west of Moscow. Kandl, who herself grew up in a quarter of Vienna that was under Soviet occupation between 1945 and 1955, remembers the anecdotes circulating about the 'Russians' when she was a child, although the occupying forces had long since left. In these accounts, the Russians were always mysterious figures. In the ongoing 'Wünsdorf Project', comprising paintings, photographs and installations, Kandl focuses on life in the enclave and the resettlement of the soldiers and their families, whom she accompanied back to Russia. Her works capture both the Russians' way of life in Germany and their encounters with the Germans, especially the way they gradually opened up to the locals, as well as life after their arrival in Russia. But the works also reflect the artist's own role and position during the process of approaching an essentially foreign – yet, on account of the stories she remembers, strangely familiar – culture. In many ways, the 'Wünsdorf Project' is therefore a form of retrospective analysis of oneself, like writing an autobiography.

Untitled (In Wjasma...)
Johanna Kandl, 1999

opposite
**Untitled (The Entrance to the
Construction Site...)**
Johanna Kandl, 1999

Macedonian artist Oliver Musovik tells stories about ordinary, banal things – things he encounters in his everyday life. Told with ironic humour, the stories may seem too personal and of no importance: they are about Musovik's family, friends and neighbours. Yet they are also a careful study of the artist's surroundings, and an examination of the effects of a new political system on daily life. These autobiographical stories reflect, in many ways, present-day transitional Macedonian society, which is an incomprehensible mixture of weighty Socialist heritage, imported Western culture, open market, prejudices, criminality, shady wealth and poverty – not only material poverty, but also mental and spiritual. The overwhelming reality of life in the Balkans is seen and interpreted by Musovik, who is perfectly aware that his own biography is inseparable from the history of his contemporaries.

top and opposite
My Best Friends
Oliver Musovik, 2002

above
Neighbours
Oliver Musovik, 1999

Vlado Petruocvski (30), my best friend from elementary school. We were inseparable for eight years. Since we didn't live in the same neighbourhood, we lost sight of each other after we finished school, and in time we stopped hanging out altogether.

For several years now, Vlado has worked in my neighbourhood, first in an optics shop and now in a photo lab. Although I wear glasses, I have never bought any in his shop, or had any repaired there, and although I often take photographs, I have never had a film developed at his place.

Aleksandar Ivanov – Zuhac (31), my best childhood friend from the apartment building we both live in (at least since Koki – my first best friend – moved away). Although he still has the apartment in our building, he spends most of his time at his grandfather's house in another part of the city, so we don't see each other often. We have always had a competitive relationship, sometimes we would buy the same or similar thing and than we would quarrel over who copied whom. I think it is obvious whose sweater is older here, no?

Aleksandar Popovski (32), my best friend from the Faculty. He graduated before me, and returned home to Bitola, a city in the south of Macedonia, where he still lives and works. We try to stay in touch as often as possible, we phone each other occasionally, and when he visits Skopje we always meet, and the same goes for when I visit Bitola.

Dejan Spasovik (28), my best friend from the Faculty during my last two years as an undergraduate. We've been discovering conceptual art together. We have even conceived several joint projects which, except for a dozen poems, we've never executed. Over time we have developed different interests and now, although we are still friends, we do not hang out that often.

Hristina Ivanoska (28), who I became friends with in 1998 in an artists' colony. For a couple of years we worked together on a foundation project. Recently, she got together with a boyfriend I openly dislike (he has the same feelings for me). This has become a problem for Hristina and me, and as a result of this we are growing apart and do not confide in each other like we used to.

My Best Friends
Oliver Musovik, 2002

**My Best Friends
(installation view)**
Oliver Musovik, 2002

In the video work *Intervista*, Albanian artist Anri Sala revisits and reconstructs a part of his mother's past, which can be considered part of his own story as well. Sala's mother was politically active in Communist Albania, and Sala confronts her with an old documentary film that shows her side by side with former Communist dictator Enver Hoxha. The sound has disappeared from the tape, but Sala has restored the lost voices with the help of lip-readers. Together with a mother who cannot or does not wish to remember this part of her life, Sala delves back into the past. He meets several people from his mother's past and asks them to talk about their memories. The video records the process of recollecting, and it brings to light what has been suppressed. The past is reconstructed through the different points of view of the participants. The film also helps Sala confront his own suppressed past. It addresses the conflict between mother and son, their relationship with each other, and their common struggle over the status of political history in private life.

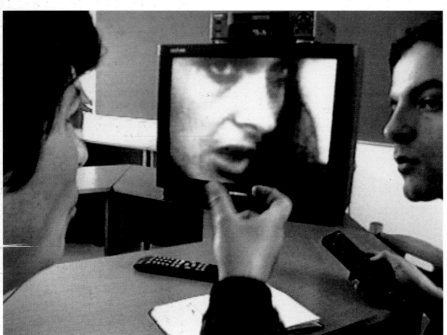

Intervista
Anri Sala, 1998

the importance of a people's
revolutionary movement.

Intervista
Anri Sala, 1998

..."against imperialism
and the two superpowers..."

Intervista
Anri Sala, 1998

MEDIA

Film, televison, magazines – we are all confronted all the time with images and ideals to aspire to. They are how we form our sense of who we are, and who we would like to be. Imagined identities are constituted by mass-media images to such an extent that escaping their influence seems to be impossible.

The starting-point of Austrian artist Dorit Margreiter's work is the part played by television in establishing identities, particularly those programmes and series that stereotype identities according to gender, class and economic position. In *Short Hills* – a video work developed over a number of years – she uses members of her own family as her subjects, specifically the family of her Chinese aunt, who moved from Hong Kong to the United States in 1972. 'Short Hills' is the name of the home of her Chinese relatives in New Jersey, but at the same time the house itself and its furniture and décor could also be the perfect setting for one of the many American soap operas. And indeed, when Margreiter's relatives are invited to tell their life stories on video, the direct influence of American and Chinese soap operas and sitcoms on their imagined identities becomes obvious. The autobiographical details recounted, the invented personalities of Margreiter's relatives, and their ideas about life, as revealed over and over again in their conversations, are clearly shaped by the example of television and the media.

Short Hills
Dorit Margreiter, 1999–2000

'My absolute favourite series is *Buffy the Vampire Slayer*. Buffy has been chosen to chase vampires and save the world and stuff. I love this series! It is funny and exciting, and the characters don't have to struggle with problems like in *Dawson's Creek*. The plot is completely unrealistic, but has a certain lightness to it. In the current season, Buffy is in her first year in college, so she is about 18 years old. Her friends help her to fight the demons, to save the world. All that is happening parallel to her "normal life", but that too is her normal life.'
Melissa Chang, Short Hills

Short Hills
Dorit Margreiter, 2000

'I have enough rooms here. One in which I sleep, another for work, and one more in addition. For some time I had a very small room, and then everything was in it – books, projects, just about everything. For a while you lie in bed and you've got your work near you, reach out to the left, and when you don't feel like it any more, you just go back to sleep. Then you realize that it's absolutely necessary at least to separate your bedroom from your work.'

'Two of you can easily work in my place. My problem is that I can't move from the area, which would often be quite a nice thing to do. During periods of intensive work it's actually pleasant and economical to work that way, but all the same you're still sitting in the same place, of course, and you've got the feeling that you're losing contact with the outside world.'

'At first it was a complete disaster. I was sharing a 20m^2 flat with a colleague – two mattresses, and a long way from the town centre. I wanted to keep improving on this situation, to get something bigger and brighter. My dream is still to have an attic apartment, where I can look out over the town.'

'I haven't got a studio but I share my workroom with Christian, at his place, because he's got a computer and I haven't. What I really like about it is that there's continual interchange, being in an office where I'm working with someone but can also withdraw again if I want to work on my own.'

Soap operas often start with a close-up of the city or building where the stories take place. In *Studiocity*, Margreiter shows 'establishing shots' that would normally locate the story in a particular place. But she does not show us the soap operas that follow these shots: in between the close-ups the screen remains blue. Instead, voices from famous actors and actresses tell us autobiographical stories about the reality of people's living conditions and their desires.

**Short Hills
(installation view)**
Dorit Margreiter, 1999–2000

@mp (asiatic mode of production)
Ruby Sircar, 2002

Working in the belief that the ethnic identity of second-generation Indian immigrants living in the West is mainly defined through images of 'Indian-ness' projected via mass-media forms such as Bollywood or Hindi movies, the half-Indian and half-German artist Ruby Sircar uses images from these sources in her art. Sircar does not therefore appear in her work, and so one might reasonably ask, how then can her art be autobiographical? But for the artist, the figures she uses, such as famous actresses, describe her own personal experience. For she would look to these stars on the screen as a link to her cultural background and her family back in India. The gridded nets over the works, which somehow systematize and give form to the idea of the Indian woman, can be read as the artist's attempt to map her own identity from the photographs. Of course, these images are not only related to Sircar's autobiography: they also function as identification models for other diaspora Indian women from her generation, who see in the actresses images of what the 'ideal' Indian woman should be, and therefore how they should act if they are to preserve the ethnic heritage of their community – something Sircar herself doubts.

@mp (asiatic mode of production)
Ruby Sircar, 2002

Love teases the brain to think and thinking makes a woman old.

top
@mp (asiatic mode of production)
Ruby Sircar, 2002

@mp (asiatic mode of production)
(installation view)
Ruby Sircar, 2001

Rosemarie Trockel looks back on popular cultural developments and their influence on the formation of the self. In works such as *Untitled (PARIS Blonde and the BB-Buch)*, Trockel examines the phenomenon of Brigitte Bardot – BB – and her huge influence upon the young women of the 1950s, in particular upon Trockel's elder sister and herself. The blonde actress BB became a shining example for a whole generation. Trockel watched her sister transform herself in Bardot's image, dyeing her hair and dressing like the star. In her work, Trockel emphasizes the emancipatory inspiration of BB. She links Bardot with another BB, the avant-garde German playwright Berthold Brecht, designing a book cover for Brecht's *Mother Courage* bearing a photograph of Bardot. But Trockel also incorporates her own autobiography into the work by, for instance, inserting an old photo of herself in the picture of her elder sister's room.

Untitled
Rosemarie Trockel, 1993

'[...] she (Brigitte Bardot) functions as a role model for all kinds of things. And yet she constantly deconstructs her own roles, although not always in a very reflective or conscious way. [...] So, the question of the model in terms of what engagement could mean these days is contradictory and ambiguous. It is also affected by our points of view. Models are a matter of one's own work. There is no model for how to deal with a model. One is never on firm ground.'

Rosemarie Trockel

'When you realize how hard it is
to know the truth about yourself,
you understand that even the most
exhaustive and well-meaning
autobiography, determined to tell
the truth, represents, at best, a guess.
There have been times in my life
when I felt incredibly happy.
Life was full. I seemed productive.
Then I thought, "Am I really happy
or am I merely masking a deep
depression with frantic activity?"
If I don't know such basic things
about myself, who does?'
Phyllis Rose

SELF-REFLECTION

Autobiography must always entail looking into the mirror of oneself and one's life. But try to grasp the reflections in that mirror – the fragile truths of one's own story – and they will often slip just out of reach.

From 1972, Friedl Kubelka embarked on her *Year Portraits*, in which, at five-yearly intervals, she attempted to find the essence of her own identity. Her first attempt at this pictorial 'self-reflection' was *1st Year's Portrait, 1972–73, 'Mirror'*, in which she set out to take a new photo of herself every day. (The gaps show that she was not able to fulfil this resolution completely.) For a whole year, she moved in front of the camera as if it were her intimate companion and, with the support of an automatic shutter release, recorded her own facial expression, with all its changing moods and emotions. In doing so, she did not stick to a single pose or camera angle, which might have resulted in greater objectivity; on the contrary, an important feature of her procedure was the way her different moods affected the daily choice and manner of self-presentation in front of the camera. It is as if the latter delivers a kind of renewed daily report on the state of mind of the subject, who must go on indefinitely reformulating her identity.

At first, the photographic act had a mainly therapeutic function. Before Kubelka started with the project she had a great reluctance to show self-portraits: she was frightened of exposing traits of her character that she wanted to hide. The *Year Portraits* were meant as a daily exercise to overcome inner barriers and to look closer at the character transported by images. At the same time, Kubelka succeeded in building up a personal archive and a visual autobiography. The project was later extended to include images of her daughter and mother.

1st Year's Portrait, 1972–73, 'Mirror' (detail)
Friedl Kubelka, 1972–73

1st Year's Portrait, 1972–73, 'Mirror' (detail)
Friedl Kubelka, 1972–73

Austrian artist Moira Zoitl deals with different roles and biographies of women, including herself. In her work, she mixes self-experienced, historically reconstructed and media-transported elements. In 2001, she reconstructed the 'Zimmer der Dame' (Lady's Room), a room designed and built in 1930 by the architect Adolf Loos for a house in Prague, in which to show her video piece *I was 0.doc*. The work is about the artist's memories of the first two decades of her life. Besides her transformation through these years, what emerges is how one's memories are constructed and how certain recollections survive, even after many years, and constantly resurface to impinge on one's self-consciousness. By placing the work within the 'Zimmer der Dame', a room specially designed for ladies, Zoitl was linking her own autobiography and her sense of self with conventional ideas of what constitutes the feminine.

I was 0.doc
Moira Zoitl, 2001

**I was 0.doc
(installation views)**
Moira Zoitl, 2001

In another video and installation, *base mix*, Zoitl talks to her mother Gloria, who is also an artist, about life as a woman, from the perspective of their own mother-daughter relationship. The interview is based on a mixture of Gloria Zoitl's biography and quotes from other women artists of the same generation (born around 1945), such as Valie Export, Carolee Schneeman and Chris Reinecke. The combination of fragments of her mother's real experiences and fictive constructions of how she could have lived turns out to be representative of the lives of women of this generation. And, as in *I was 0.doc*, we find a reciprocal construction between personal autobiography and social roles – yet again representative of women's experience in our society.

Professoren verfügten über eine

base mix
Moira Zoitl, 1998

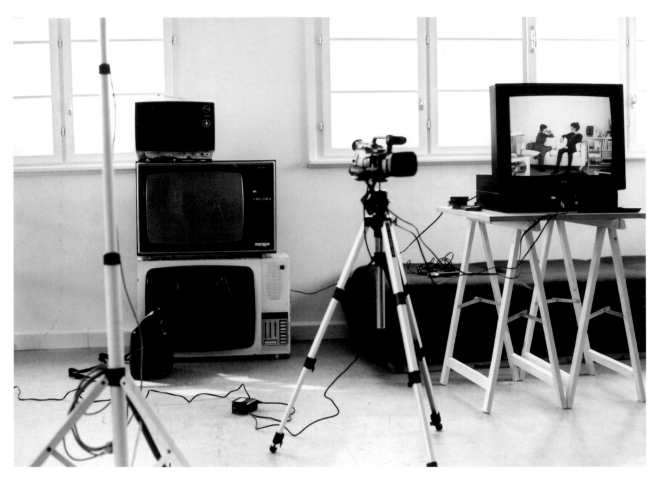

base mix (set photo)
Moira Zoitl, 1998

base mix
Moira Zoitl, 1998

**Self-portrait on the rocks,
Levanzo, Sicily**

Nan Goldin, 1999

opposite, above
Jens' hand on Clemens' back, Paris

Nan Goldin, 2001

opposite, below
**Valerie in the light,
Bruno in the dark, Paris**

Nan Goldin, 2001

'Since my early teens, I'd lived by an Oscar Wilde saying, that you are who you pretend to be.'
Nan Goldin

In 1972, American artist Nan Goldin began to photograph a number of her friends who had made a conscious effort to assert or even change their sexual identity: drag queens, transsexuals and transvestites. Goldin's photos tell the story of her close personal relationships with these people, with whom she lived for a period, and they also record social breakthroughs in the United States, and instances of acceptance, ignorance and rejection. Furthermore, they capture the transience of life, rescuing it from collective and individual forgetfulness. Triggered by cases of AIDS and a series of deaths, Goldin's photos form a kind of memory bank – a storehouse of alternative, individualistic images giving visible existence to, and asserting the continued presence of, communities that have been marginalized and discriminated against.

For the last thirty years Goldin has continued to photograph her friends. The images also reflect Goldin's own life, in that they chart her photographic journey from its beginnings in Boston, through stays in Manila and Bangkok, where she photographed male prostitutes and homosexual culture, to present-day Paris, where she has photographed friends, often with their children.

Cross in the fog, Brides-les-Bains, France
Nan Goldin, 2002

'One of my closest friends in the pictures from the '70s died a few years ago and one of the beauties in the recent pictures, a few weeks ago. Due in large part to the AIDS crisis, the attitudes of my friends in the '90s have shifted. The previous glorification of the glamour of self-destruction and substance abuse has been replaced with a will to survive.'

Nan Goldin

Fatima candles, Portugal
Nan Goldin, 1998

'To accept life in all its recurrent horror means to go beyond ... notions of judgment, beyond good and bad, before and after. This is the only way we can finally be free.'

Guido Costa

opposite and page 182
from the series 'Lad'
Wiebke Loeper, 1996–97

East German artist Wiebke Loeper works with the memory of her childhood and youth. In *MOLL 31* (1995), she recalled her family life in one of the many *Plattenbaus* (prefabricated buildings made from concrete slabs) that were common in the former GDR, and which came to represent social progress and a strong belief in the country's glorious future. She juxtaposed family photos taken by her father in the 1970s with her own shots of the same places in the present day: for example, a picture of a bathtub in which Loeper is playing alongside the same wall decades later where almost all the tiles have fallen off. In *Lad*, Loeper visited the most significant sites of her childhood in East Berlin: the kindergarten, the school, the supermarket. In the resulting photographs and text pieces, she deals with the disappearance of the past and its recollection in memory. Loeper grew up in a country that no longer exists; not only have the objects and scenes of her childhood disappeared, but also the ideals of that time have lost their value too. She asks, how far can places and things reproduce memory, and how far do present images overlap with the past in the construction of one's self? Where does one's autobiography ultimately reside?

'Each autobiographical memory … is part of a personal narrative, which reflects our views of ourselves…. They represent the current "life style" of the individual, and serve to remind the person of who he or she is…. Childhood memories don't determine adult personality; rather adult personality determines what will be remembered from childhood.'

John F. Kihlstrom

Lad is a Plattdeutsch (Low German) word meaning a trunk that holds the most important household goods (e.g. documents, valuables, heirlooms, crockery, linen etc.) and is used by people escaping from fire, flood, war etc.

I assumed that I had grown up with things from the seventies and eighties. This may have been true of food and clothing, but not of everyday objects. Their intellectual origins went back to the twenties, the time of the 'Bauhaus', and their design and technology stemmed from the sixties. Later social norms – embodied by wall units, interior designs and all sorts of temporary things – influenced every aspect of furnishing. In this way my generation – this is my view – got to know very few objects that fitted in with their own time. But in a certain way they did correspond to it, because in political life too there were no innovative developments.

Furniture and utensils will sooner or later end up on the rubbish dump. This gives every generation the liberty to start again from scratch. But do I want this 'liberty'? In fact do I actually have a choice? With the demolition and change of the structured environment, does my hereditary right of domicile disappear?

My father's drawing fascinated me even when I was a child. It shows no fear of future design. When I was given the task of creating a picture of the future, I didn't know what to do.

Motor racing circuit, parents' house, dining room, friend, girlfriend, hotel, courtyard, institute, Kamelit, department store, cellar, kindergarten teacher, kindergarten, cinema, clinic, crib, park, pioneer republic, doll, doll's house, school, school corridor, school playground, swimming pool, swimming instructor, playground, tablecloth, tabletop, stairwell, gymnasium, changing room, wall, water sports, residential area …

My father's picture of the year 2000, drawn in 1960, when he was 18 years old.

I would like to have rooms that radiate the security of my childhood, for example a cupboard in which I could sit, and on whose inner substance of time and continuity I would feed – a cupboard that would possess an inner form. Where we lived there was only one modular construction unit which fell apart and formed new pieces of furniture when we moved house. We didn't take secure rooms with us.

I was born in Buch Clinic, in House 103. I went to the place several times, in order to visit someone or to undergo examinations myself. I didn't quite know in which of these many similar houses I'd been born. Also I couldn't find the house in which I'd visited my mother for the last time. One day I thought I could really settle on a particular one. But when my father told me that I entered the world in House 103, I stood in front of the house and wasn't sure any more – I had the feeling there'd been a mistake.

TALK

Bart de Baere, Ilina Koralova, Julia Schäfer, B, J, S, Y

THE MYTH OF AUTOBIOGRAPHY

Y: May I begin by asking about the choice of artists who appear in this book? Because it seems to me to be missing some key figures who dealt with, or deal with, autobiographical questions. For example Joseph Beuys. The use of felt and fat in many of his art works has a definite autobiographical significance. During the Second World War, Beuys's fighter plane crashed over the Crimea. Nomadic Tartars found him and wrapped his body in felt and fat, thus saving his life. He referred to this experience time and again in his art.

J: Do you know why Beuys doesn't belong to our selection? Because he really believes there is such a thing as an authentic life story and a definable identity. The way he tells his own story is very linear. He believes in the possibility of coherent autobiography.

BdB: Actually, research done in the last few years has uncovered hard proof that the Tartar story is a myth, which only reaffirms your remarks because the story reinforces the coherence of this individual mythology. The story still wants to be believed.

B: We have deliberately chosen artistic positions that question the authenticity of autobiography. In some cases we find works that pretend to be authentic but turn out to be totally infected by mass media. Take Elke Krystufek: a lot of people feel a voyeuristic attraction on watching her re-enactment of 'private' acts, such as the masturbation she performed at the Kunsthalle in Vienna (page 85). But the point is that everything is staged for the public. Krystufek once said that she feels quite sad that she completely lacks privacy. She has been a public figure from a very early age – omnipresent in media and influenced by media herself. Another example: Tracey Emin. We can never know how 'true' her apparently real-life confessions are, however often they are repeated on talk shows, or in magazines and newspapers. You can't know if Emin really ever slept in the bed that was exhibited at the Tate Gallery. Nor can you

draw the line between fact and fiction in Sophie Calle's work. She lived strictly according to concepts that she devised herself, or that others proposed. The novelist Paul Auster, inspired by the artist, created a character – Maria – after Calle. Later Calle adopted Maria and lived the life Auster wrote for her. Every artist in this book is fully aware of the constructed nature of all autobiography.

We have deliberately chosen artistic positions that question the authenticity of autobiography.

JS: Moira Zoitl's video work *base mix* also fits into our discussion. Zoitl questions the idea that we each have our 'own life' as something that exists independently of public life, social conventions, aesthetic ideals, etc. For her, every biography is inevitably defined by those parameters. 'No such thing as an abstract self exists. This imagination is a male myth,' she says. *Base mix* is a discussion between Zoitl and her mother, the artist Gloria Zoitl. It relates the life-story of her mother – but actually this is not only Gloria's story, it is the story of all women of her generation. The mother integrates the words of other women into the report of her 'own' life without acknowledgment.

IK: Another piece by Zoitl, *I was 0.doc*, confirms what you say. Zoitl's way of remembering her first twenty years turns out to be a model for many women who grew up in that society. It's a construction of personal memories which have common currency. At the same time, this work shows the unpredictable nature of what stays in your mind – what lasts.

JS: I think Zoitl's works touch on important questions: how did women live, how strongly were their lives influenced by society and its norms, and how would their lives have unfolded in other times?

IK: Adrian Piper's work seems to be symptomatic of that as well. She speaks from the point of view of an artist but also from that of a black woman. She addresses social discrimination and describes her personal situation.

B: She has always been between two groups – white and black Americans. She has a very pale face and you could easily fail to recognize her negroid features. This fact has caused her enormous tension in her life.

No such thing as an abstract self exists. This imagination is a male myth.

S: The feeling of being 'in between' also leads us to a group of artists who grew up with different cultural backgrounds. It seems that they are especially aware of the fact that autobiography has a lot to do with construction. Am I right?

J: You are right, because their identity, or self-image, is constantly challenged through the experience of different cultural backgrounds. Therefore it is not fixed. And quite often insecurity comes in, which again produces a permanent shift and questioning of 'who one is'. When the Öztürks and Jun Yang reconstruct their childhood and youth, they themselves can't remember how it really was. Only vague memories, stories told by others or clichéd images taken out of movies generate an image of their own autobiography. They were simply too young when they left their countries. But this constant search for identity is not limited to artists who come out of a mixed cultural background. You can find it in many other artists' work as well. That's why in the title of the introduction we focused on the impermanence of identity. Creating an autobiography always means writing identity, and it also means constantly redefining identity.

IK: If I may add something, 'redefining identity' is a very important issue for the artists working in Eastern Europe nowadays. Take the examples of Oliver Musovik from Macedonia, Anri Sala from Albania or RASSIM® from Bulgaria. What has been going on in these countries for ten years is the redefinition of the image of the artist. What's more, it's searching for a new identity, not only within the artistic field but in general.

J: But do you think that is authentic?

IK: Well, come on, we all know that in those countries the influence of media images is quite strong, and of course this influences the idea of oneself a lot, especially if there is a weak or shaky social situation. In such circumstances, you are urgently looking for appropriate role models. So many ideas have come and gone in recent years in the post-Socialist countries. You can see that with RASSIM®. The image he adopted in 2001 has disappeared. Nowadays it looks a little bit ridiculous, don't you think?

J: Well, I thought it was always meant to be a sort of parody.

IK: You can't be sure about that. That's what I like. You simply don't know if the artist believes in such a role model or if he's making fun of it.

Creating an autobiography always means creating identity, and it also means constantly redefining identity.

B: During our research we found some artistic positions that start with the myth of an authentic biography, like Christian Boltanski's. You believe in the authenticity of his photographs, which illustrate his childhood, but in fact they come from different sources. The authentic autobiography not only becomes a myth; the myth itself becomes a subject of the work. But it is exactly that myth which makes works and artists attractive. To read an artist's autobiography suggests an almost intimate knowledge of the person behind it. The fallacy is to think that by looking at an 'autobiographical work' one is seeing the artist speaking authentically.

J: Yes, but playing with authenticity might help to make people listen.

JS: I agree. Antje Schiffers' trips are appealing because she suggests that she was 'really' with the people, staying in their houses, eating and drinking with them. And some of the countries she visits, such as Russia, Kazakhstan and Kirghizia, could look very exotic to visitors to her exhibitions or to readers of her books. Her position can be compared with that of an ethnographer, but nowadays we all know that ethnographers don't just watch from a distance: they influence a situation and project their own ideas on the object of examination. And in Schiffers' case, of course, the people she lives with are not that isolated. Some watch TV, some read books and newspapers, and they tell the news stories to others. But Schiffers plays with the idea of the authentic travel report, which, by the way, has become a genre of its own, having a certain form and language. Like a live report, her personal diary was published in a German newspaper while she was still travelling.

BdB: I like the oscillation between something that has an aura of truth on the one hand and dubiousness on the other. It creates a special watchfulness. It urges for the proposal to be considered as possible *meaning*, not as possible *truth* or information. But that only comes about when an artist generates this oscillation, and is very careful about both being truthful and revealing the construction of the story. A good example, I feel, is how the Belgian artist Jan Vercruysse changes his birthplace from biography to biography. It is not where he's born that becomes important, but the gradual construction of a cultural horizon, in which Elisabethville in Belgian Congo is as important a reference as Ostend. As references, these fragments are probably more relevant than the place in which he was really born, if it is any of those places.

J: I like the idea of being closer to a certain reality through construction.

S: But what if the story that is told gets really existential? I mean, artists who suffer, who question themselves … you know, there are tragic figures. If you look at their pieces, you can't be in any doubt of that. What about Nan Goldin? Her autobiography is unavoidably linked with those of her friends, and many of these friends died of AIDS. Photography preserves their memory, preserves their image, at least. And what about Martin Kippenberger? His posters show a vulnerable person, despite the fact that he made fun of society and of himself. That is truly melancholic!

B: In the section 'Self-Reflection', we included Nan Goldin, Moira Zoitl, Friedl Kubelka and Wiebke Loeper.

J: We decided on them because we had a strong interest in their self-questioning, their self-mirroring. From the 1970s onwards, Kubelka took a photograph of herself almost every day. The images show a wide range of feelings – the happy person, the unlucky one, the person who is struggling with herself, who is getting older, who looks sceptically into her mirror, and so on.

The authentic autobiography not only becomes a myth; the myth itself becomes a subject of the work.

B: Wiebke Loeper deals with her past. She grew up in East Germany, a country that has now gone. But she feels part of her identity has also gone with it. Of course she doesn't want East Germany back, but she is interested in the traces of the past, both within herself and in the outside world; she is interested in the effects of that past on her present identity. A lot of people, especially younger ones, the ones born in the 1970s, struggle with the loss of the past that influenced them when they were children. So Loeper examines in her work the remains of what has gone. Of course, that is also tragic. But on the other hand it is not about searching for an authentic past. She knows perfectly well that images of the past constantly overlap with images of the present, with things that have happened since the end of Communism, and with media images. And her work is about those phenomena as well.

Y: The longer I think about our discussion on authenticity, the more I am convinced that the interest of viewers and readers actually has more to do with personification – with celebrating the 'individual'. And artists are, for many, the last true individuals in the world, and therefore representatives of tragic lives. Only the authentic person feels real pain; other people simply don't know what it means to suffer. I would like to call that the Van Gogh effect! Even if artists tell really touching stories, even if they are true, I can't shake off the feeling that all this feeds hidden voyeuristic needs. It is about curiosity as well. To really find out … to talk about … sorry to say this, but I see it as a sort of gossiping on a more advanced level.

B: I agree to a certain point. The belief in an authentic speaker produces a feeling of participating in the life of someone else, or of sharing intimate moments. But the artists know about these mechanisms and they exploit them. And anyway, just because something turns out to be essential for an artist or anyone else does not mean that it has to be authentic. It can be constructed as well. We are talking about effects! Even constructed things can cause strong, essential effects.

J: The artists in our book play with the desire of the viewer or the reader to be close. Actually they turn voyeurism around. Take Rirkrit Tiravanija: he didn't exhibit his real apartment in Cologne but a life-size model. Even when people lived there for a while, its construction *as a model* always remained visible.

Y: We are talking a lot about authenticity, the construction of autobiography: what about artists who delegate their autobiography to 'somebody else'? I mean, they seem to reject any kind of focus on the subject, on their 'real' persona.

S: You mean those artists who construct 'alter egos', who live another life?

Y: Yes. If we take Eleanor Antin, then the starting-point is apparently a feminist one. She slips into various characters – the male super ego, which is the king, and the black prima ballerina or the caring nurse, both of which can be seen as ideal female figures.

B: In her case, she created different figures that all seem to fail somehow in the moment they act. As long as one looks at their photos, everything seems to be perfect; they seem to be fulfilling the idea of their own characters. But look more closely and you see them slipping up – the ballerina, for example, who is supported by props. One can also see something similar happening in relation to autobiography itself. Telling a coherent story is doomed to failure. But as long as you look at the surface of an autobiographical story it looks coherent. It's when you look closer that the myth collapses.

S: What about Anita Leisz? Her figure Den Rest exists only on a conceptual level. Den Rest is separated from the artist's life, having his own identity – or, more correctly, his own different identities. Actually he is an elusive character: you can't describe him, can't really 'get' him.

J: Roberta Breitmore, the character created by Lynn Hershman, also had an identity of her own. During the ten years of Breitmore's existence, she managed to get her own driving licence and credit card. In both cases, in Leisz's work and Hershman's, the obvious construction of the characters is linked to the construction of an autobiography.

To read an artist's autobiography suggests an almost intimate knowledge of the person behind it. The fallacy is to think that by looking at an 'autobiographical work' one is seeing the artist speaking authentically.

IK: Apparently, the creation of 'alter egos' or 'fictitious characters' is a subject many artists are interested in. We can add to the list the name of Oliver Hangl and his character Daniel Rose. Hangl felt very much inspired by a Woody Allen movie, where the character slipped out of the screen and acted like a real person. Later Hangl gave up Daniel Rose and created a double of his own. In the 'Stereo Pieces', both appear: Hangl and the double. From a certain standpoint their faces and bodies overlap and they can no longer be separated visually.

B: I see the 'alter ego' as a kind of 'protecting' of one's character and, at the same time, as quite a powerful tool to talk about personal things.

S: Well, dealing with alter egos always seems to be a case of 'split personae'. Look at Oliver Hangl! That's how you end up!

B: Come on now, you shouldn't mix up fiction and reality. Hangl is not a split personality at all, he just plays with multiple characters. Look at it like this: the alter egos offer the possibility of talking about oneself indirectly. It has nothing to do with the disintegration of a person through multiplicity. In this context, Warhol seems to be much more interesting. There are so many images of 'Andy Warhol' from other people's projections. He pretended not to exist as a person in his own right; he pretended not to have a memory. In an interview, he would say, 'You give me the answers – and I'll repeat them' or, at a different point, 'I have no memory.' Actually Warhol didn't have his own biography. It was constantly produced by others.

Artists are, for many, the last true individuals in the world, and therefore representatives of tragic lives. Only the authentic person feels real pain; other people simply don't know what it means to suffer. I would like to call that the Van Gogh effect!

S: Warhol is not the only artist whose autobiography can't be grasped. Take Jeff Koons or Cindy Sherman.

JS: This is really interesting! If you take Koons's designed autobiography and the changing appearance of Cindy Sherman, you can easily link their way of dealing with their public lives with that of pop stars, who want to protect themselves from the public. With each new album, Madonna, for example, produces a totally new image of herself. Her autobiography is an ongoing metamorphosis. And with each image she influences others' lives. But talking about 'alter egos' and 'doubles' and 'split personalities', I would also like to mention Björk's way of creating her autobiography. In public, she exists more and more as a digital version and a robot – a disappearing figure. This allows the private Björk to live an independent life running parallel to that of the pop star 'Björk'.

B: Koons's biography has been developed to suit his perfect image. In his case, we are dealing with an absolutely designed autobiography. We can't even say if his marriage to the porn star La Cicciolina was calculated from a career point of view or if it was true love. Maybe both.

Y: At least they have a child together! And I guess that was not part of the designed autobiography.

B: How can you be sure? I remember gossip in 1991 when people suspected something like that.

Y: Meanwhile there are fights going on about who should raise the child. It hurts Koons obviously; he really suffers a lot.

BdB: Now I would like to know, isn't that the case with many other artists' biographies? I mean the fact that artists fake their personal data. I am thinking of faked birthdays or careers. It helps to support the image of a successful artist. So couldn't we say that every biography is constructed to impress or to mystify?

B: In comparison to these 'manipulations', Koons goes further; he makes an artistic subject out of it. And that's an important difference.

BdB: It seems to me that your idea of art is quite limited, like a binary yes/no. Haven't artists made consciously artistic gestures both within and outside completely formulated areas of attention for years, the ones we might label as artistic objects or artistic subjects? Ways of being present or absent at social events, for example.

S: Let's come back to the disappearance of autobiography. What about disappearance by accumulation – accumulation of images of the past (Christian Boltanski), accumulation of 'roles' (Cindy Sherman), or accumulation of 'facts' (On Kawara, Mary Kelly)?

BdB: Super interesting. Because at first you don't see those positions in relation to autobiography. You miss the subject.

S: Yes, but that is the point. Writing an autobiography is not necessarily connected to a strong subject.

B: The disappearance of autobiography, as you call it – I would prefer 'dissolution of autobiography' – has indeed played an important role in our thoughts. We understood it as an intrinsic part of our subject. You can't think about autobiography without taking into consideration all the artists who consciously refuse to have a biography, or whose biography can't be grasped.

J: This leads us again to On Kawara's 'Date Paintings', in which he uses different styles of writing the date depending on his location. Or the work *I read*, in which he registers all the newspaper articles he has read worldwide during a certain period of time. In his case, the notes remain purely factual – no personal emotion … or to put it differently, the emotion is not visible; it is covered by a minute system.

BdB: May I intervene? Emotion could also come in despite one using those rational recording systems. This is the important difference between On Kawara and Mary Kelly. The latter uses already existing standardized modes to register life, but at the same time – and here lies the difference to Kawara's work – she interferes subjectively and adds personal notes. The tension between subjectivity and objectivity also plays an important role in Richter's *Atlas*. It consists of images taken out of the mass media and private photographs of his friends and family. His autobiography is put in relation to worldwide events. Subjectively produced and publicly published material stand side by side.

B: But do you know what was really difficult? We could not convince On Kawara to participate in our book. He refused to be in a book on autobiography. I guess his understanding of autobiography implies a strong involvement with the subject.

Y: Do you think the disappearance/dissolution of autobiography means a conscious refusal of a strong subject position? The use of registration and protocol systems is in complete contrast to the subjective approach of writing an autobiography.

J: I would say those positions question a certain understanding of subjectivity. And that is important for our understanding of autobiography. I still think that On Kawara's is an especially interesting position in the context of autobiography.

S: What is highly interesting with Kawara, Kelly and Richter is that they use formats which are usually used in, and refer to, other social contexts – the protocol system, the scientific diagram, the archive. But this feature is just more obvious in their work. I think any autobiography is embedded within a larger political, economic, social and cultural context, and therefore refers to other fields.

You should not mix up fiction and reality. Alter egos offer the possibility of talking about oneself indirectly. It has nothing to do with the disintegration of a person through multiplicity.

J: That's one of the starting-points of Adrian Piper, who we've talked about already. Her experiences of being a 'woman', an 'artist' and a member of a 'black minority' in the US put her in a position to regard telling and writing 'autobiography' not solely as something personal but also as a political statement…

IK: … which applies also to the South African Tracey Rose, who was classified during apartheid as 'coloured' (mixed race). Her works may seem very personal, but they are so much about being physically and mentally trapped, about terror and violence.… It's also a sort of role-playing, but completely different from Cindy Sherman. Rose slips into roles that are either inaccessible to black people or else the complete opposite: clichés. The black revue girl, for instance. Everybody immediately thinks of Josephine Baker. This image has influenced us so much!

J: It seems that living in South Africa encourages a strong critical approach to the political context. And of course it has side effects for the artist's autobiography. William Kentridge crosses my mind. He is a white artist who deals with the situation in South Africa and links the socio-political situation with his autobiography. His figures are related to his family history as well as to the socio-political developments after apartheid. There is the capitalist Soho

Eckstein, who has similar features to Kentridge's grandfather, and the dreamer of a better world, Felix Teitlebaum, who is like the artist himself.

BdB: The stronger the political circumstances the artists are in, the stronger the discrimination they feel; and the more oppressed they feel, the more it has a strong impact on their lives. And the moment they start talking about their lives, they talk about the political circumstances too. That's not at all surprising! Many artists who lived or live under restrictive regimes talk about that. Ilya Kabakov dealt with the Soviet system…

B: Yes, you're right, but it's not only about living under political limitations. The politically 'in-between' situations seem to be just as interesting for artists. In *Intervista*, Anri Sala deals with Albania's post-Communist era. His starting-point is a coincidental moment: the discovery of an old film roll featuring his mother, which led him to reconstruct his mother's biography, which is linked to the history of Albania and to his own biography. Sala starts with a personal story, his mother's, but takes up a documentary mode, suggesting an objective approach.

The stronger the political circumstances the artists are in, the stronger the discrimination they feel; and the more oppressed they feel, the more it has a strong impact on their lives.

JS: But don't you think it just depends on the interest of an artist? Some are more interested in political systems than others. Take Johannes Wohnseifer. He consciously tells his autobiography in parallel to the history of West Germany. He mixes up personal anecdotes, snapshots of his friends and his childhood photos with groundbreaking political events, the attacks by the RAF, famous design objects, lifestyle, movies, in fact anything that influenced his identity. The individual story is inseparable from the collective one.

J: Wohnseifer uses a lot of media images he cuts out of magazines and newspapers. And that leads to another aspect of autobiography – the role and influence of mass media on building identity and the self-portrait that is developed in an autobiography. We already picked up on it briefly but I would like to discuss the role of TV and movies in more detail.

BdB: In the heyday of political correctness, David Hammons played in a very ambiguous way with autobiographical facts and with being pinned down by a token Afro-American position. He had to, because the very specificity he was offering could only work on an equal footing, not if it was categorized from the beginning. The media aspect – how one looks at indigenous people – had an impact on Hammons.

The individual story is inseparable from the collective one.

B: Well, that's important with all cultures that are perceived as exotic. Dorit Margreiter deals with that subject – among other aspects, of course. She asked her Chinese mother to read the trendy book *Women of the Orient* – a real mass product, that is to say – which is full of prejudices. Margreiter filmed her mother and announced her reading on a movie poster: 'Elaine Tak Yee Margreiter reading the book, camera and editing done by Dorit Margreiter'. The artist wanted to show the construction of the 'nature' attributed to Chinese women. And she made fun out of it. The mother is reading a ridiculous book like that without batting an eyelid.

JS: It seems that female artists are especially sensitive to media phenomena and their effects on the constitution of identity. But it doesn't necessarily mean that they look towards the media negatively. Sometimes there is an interest in the emancipative role of the media. Take Ruby Sircar, who is half Indian and half German, and grew up in Germany. The influence of Indian mass media on her identity was very strong. For second-generation immigrants like her, mass media take the place of first-hand experiences. In her work, she focuses on the influence of Hindi and Bollywood movies on women. The singing and dancing sequences allow the women to express their dreams and to explore their independence.

J: To continue with that subject, Rosemarie Trockel looked closely at the myth of Brigitte Bardot, who was a model for many young women in the '50s. Those young women wanted to liberate themselves, they wanted to go out, they wanted to have fun and they wanted to have sex without marriage. And of course Trockel herself was one of the young girls who were influenced by BB.

B: You can't get rid of media images when you decide to write your autobiography. There is always something or somebody you saw on TV or in a movie that impresses you so much you incorporate it into your own personal history…

IK: Sometimes it is the only thing you have. Ruby Sircar was mentioned before. Mostly she had to rely on second-hand experiences. She didn't grow up in India. Of course, one could say that the media images tell you something about India, but not in terms of authenticity. Jun Yang is another good example, in his videos *from salariiman to superman*, or *coming home – daily structures of life*, where movie sequences and the stories of his life intersect. And this links us back again to the question of an authentic biography. It is a fake, but a fake that tells us a lot!

J: Perhaps, since we are at the very end of our discussion, we should reveal its underlying construction – the fact that it includes real and fictitious elements. Throughout, real curators from Antwerp, Sofia and Leipzig have been talking about real and invented artists to invented characters named after the initials J and Y (Jun Yang) and B and S (Barbara Steiner). You could compare it to 'writing an autobiography'.

B: But now everybody's going to want to know who the fictitious artists are, don't you think?

BdB: Bart de Baere is the director of the MUHKA in Antwerp

IK: Ilina Koralova is a freelance curator based in Sofia

JS: Julia Schäfer is a curator at the Galerie für Zeitgenössische Kunst in Leipzig

THE ARTISTS

ELEANOR ANTIN
b. 1935, New York (USA); lives in San Diego (USA)

Select exhibitions
Venice Biennale (group exh.), Venice, 1976
Whitney Biennial (group exh.), Whitney Museum of American Art, New York, 1989
'The American Century: Art and Culture 1900–2000' (group exh.), Whitney Museum of American Art, New York, 1999
'Eleanor Antin Retrospective' (solo exh.), Los Angeles County Museum of Art, Los Angeles, California, 1999
Sydney Biennial (group exh.), Sydney, 2002

Select publications
100 Boots Once Again, Wadsworth Atheneum (exh. cat.), Hartford, Connecticut, 1977
Antin, Eleanor, *Being Antinova*, Astro Artz, Los Angeles, California, 1983
Antin, Eleanor, *Eleanora Antinova Plays*, Sun & Moon Press, Los Angeles, California, 1994
Fox, Howard N. (ed.), *Eleanor Antin*, Los Angeles County Museum of Art (exh. cat.), Los Angeles, California, 1999
100 Boots, Running Press, Philadelphia, Pennsylvania, 1999

CHRISTIAN BOLTANSKI
b. 1944, Paris (France); lives in Paris (France)

Select exhibitions
'Documenta 8' (group exh.), Kassel, 1987
'Christian Boltanski: Dernières Années' (solo exh.), Musée d'Art Moderne de la Ville de Paris, Paris, 1998
'Ich ist etwas Anderes: Kunst am Ende des 20. Jahrhunderts' (group exh.), Kunstsammlung Nordrhein-Westfalen, Dusseldorf, 2000
'Voilà, le monde dans la tête' (group exh.), Musée d'Art Moderne de la Ville de Paris, Paris, 2000
'Dialogue ininterrompu' (group exh.), Musée des Beaux-Arts de Nantes, Nantes, 2001

Select publications
Schraenen, Guy (ed.), *'Inventar' aller Bücher verlegt zwischen 1969 und 1995 von Christian Boltanski*, Neues Museum Weserburg (exh. cat.), Bremen, 1996
Paflik-Huber, Hannelore, *Kunst und Zeit: Zeitmodelle der Gegenwartskunst*, Scaneg, Munich, 1997

Schwerfel, Heinz Peter, *Kunstskandale,* DuMont, Cologne, 2000
Eichhorn, Herbert (ed.), *KinderBlicke: Kindheit und Moderne von Klee bis Boltanski*, Hatje Cantz, Ostfildern/Stuttgart, 2001
Tableaux Vivants: Lebende Bilder und Attitüden in Fotografie, Film und Video, Kunsthalle Wien (exh. cat.), Vienna, 2002

SOPHIE CALLE
b. 1953, Paris (France); lives in Malakoff (France) and New York (USA)

Select exhibitions
'Die wahren Geschichten der Sophie Calle' (solo exh.), Museum Fridericianum, Kassel, 2000
'Sophie Calle: Public Spaces, Private Spaces' (solo exh.), The Jewish Museum San Francisco, San Francisco, 2001
'Sophie Calle: Retrospektive im Rahmen des gewonnenen Spektrum Preises 2001' (solo exh.), Sprengel Museum, Hannover, 2002
'Par le chas d'une aiguille' (group exh.), Galerie Chantal Crousel, Paris, 2003
'Sophie Calle: Double Games' (solo exh.), Paula Cooper Gallery, New York, 2003

Select publications
Heinrich, Barbara (ed.), *Die wahren Geschichten der Sophie Calle*, Kunsthalle Museum Fridericianum (exh. cat.), Kassel, 2000
Knaller, Susanne (ed.), *Zeitgenössische Allegorien: Literatur, Kunst, Theorie*, Fink, Munich, 2001
2twice: inside cars, Princeton Architectural Press, Princeton, New Jersey, 2001
Gotham Handbook, Galerie Arndt & Partner (exh. cat.), Berlin, 2002
Sophie Calle, Sprengel Museum Hannover (exh. cat.), Hannover, 2002
Sophie Calle, Walther König, Cologne, 2002

TRACEY EMIN
b. 1963, London (UK); lives in London (UK)

Select exhibitions
'Tracey Emin: Every Part of Me's Bleeding' (solo exh.), Lehmann Maupin, New York, 1999
Turner Prize (group exh.), Tate Gallery, London, 1999
'I will never let you go' (group exh.), Moderna Museet Stockholm, Stockholm, 2001
'Stories' (group exh.), Haus der Kunst, Munich, 2002
'Tracey Emin: This is Another Place' (solo exh.), The Museum of Modern Art, Oxford, 2002

Select publications
The Aggression of Beauty, Galerie Arndt & Partner (exh. cat.), Berlin, 1996
Sensation: Young British Artists from the Saatchi Collection, Thames & Hudson (exh. cat.), London, 1997
Brown, Neal (ed.), *Tracey Emin: I need art like I need God*, South London Art Gallery (exh. cat.), London, 1998
Ca – Ca Poo – Poo: Malerei nach der Organisation der Malerei, Cantz (exh. cat.), Ostfildern/Stuttgart, 2002
Townsend, Chris and Mandy Merck (eds), *The Art of Tracey Emin*, Thames & Hudson, London, 2002

NAN GOLDIN
b. 1953, Washington (USA); lives in New York (USA) and Paris (France)

Select exhibitions
'FémininMasculin: Le sexe de l'art' (group exh.), Musée national d'art moderne, Centre Georges Pompidou, Paris, 1995
Whitney Biennial (group exh.), Whitney Museum of American Art, New York, 1995
'I'll be your mirror' (solo exh.), Whitney Museum of American Art, New York; Kunstmuseum Wolfsburg; Fotomuseum Winterthur; Stedelijk Museum, Amsterdam; Kunsthalle Wien, 1996
'Social Documents' (group exh.), Los Angeles Museum of Contemporary Art, Los Angeles, California, 1996
'Nan Goldin' (solo exh.), Matthew Marks Gallery, New York, 1998

Select publications
Goldin, Nan, *The Ballad of Sexual Dependency*, Secker & Warburg, London, 1989
Goldin, Nan, *The Other Side, 1972–1992*, Scalo-Verlag, Zurich, 1992
Goldin, Nan, *Couples and Loneliness*, Korinsha Press, Kyoto, 1998
Goldin, Nan, *Memories are Made of This*, Galerie Epikur (exh. cat.), Wuppertal, 1998
Townsend, Chris, *Vile Bodies: Photography and the Crisis of Looking*, Prestel, Munich, 1998

OLIVER HANGL
b. 1968, Vienna (Austria); lives in Vienna (Austria)

Select exhibitions
'Double Fiction' (solo exh.), Kunstverein Ludwigsburg, 1998
'Hotel Very Heavy' (solo exh.), Kunsthalle Exnergasse, Vienna, 1999

'Picture This! Here and Gone' (solo exh.), Konstmuseum, Kristinehamns, Stockholm, 2001
'Lovers' Walk' (solo exh.), Museum für Angewandte Kunst, Vienna, 2003
'Picture This: Mr Rose' (solo exh.), Stadtmuseum Wels, Wels, 2003

Select publications
Time out, Kunsthalle Nürnberg (exh. cat.), Nuremberg, 1997
Art traffic / art trafik, Art Phalanx (exh. cat.), Vienna, 1999
Studiocity, Kunstverein Wolfsburg (exh. cat.), Wolfsburg, 1999
Shoot, Kunsthalle Malmö (exh. cat.), Malmö, 2000

LYNN HERSHMAN
b. 1941, Cleveland, Ohio (USA); lives in San Francisco (USA)

Select exhibitions
'Videoverk van Lynn Hershman' (solo exh.), Stelling Gallery, Leiden, 1997
'Digital Pioneers' (group exh.), Museum of Modern Art, New York, 1999
'New Works' (solo exh.), Gallery 16, San Francisco, California, 1999
'Media & Identity' (solo exh.), Sweeney Gallery, University of California, Riverside, 2000
'Hero Sandwiches' (solo exh.), University of Virginia Museum of Art, Charlottesville, 2001

Select publications
Roth, Moira (ed.), *The Amazing Decade: Women and Performance Art in America, 1970–1980*, Astro Artz, Los Angeles, 1983
Albright, Thomas, *Art in the San Francisco Bay Area, 1945–1980: An Illustrated History*, University of California Press, Berkeley, California, 1985
Hershman, Lynn, *Die Phantasie außer Kontrolle*, Kunstforum International, Ruppichteroth, Mainz, 1989
Hershman, Lynn (ed.), *Clicking In: Hot Links to a Digital Culture*, Bay Press, Seattle, Washington, 1996
Wark, Jayne, *The Radical Gesture: Feminism and Performance Art*, Roberta Breitmore's Construction Chart, 1997
Sterling, Bruce, *What difference does difference make? The difference engine revisited*, Kettle's Yard, Cambridge, 2000

CHRISTINE HILL
b. 1968, New York (USA); lives in New York (USA)

Select exhibitions
'Documenta 10' (group exh.), Kassel, 1997
Berlin Biennial (group exh.), 1998
'Urban Nomads' (group exh.), South London Gallery, London, 2001
'Christine Hill: Volksboutique Organizational Ventures' (solo exh.), Migros Museum, Zurich, 2001; Kunstverein Wolfsburg, Wolfsburg, 2001; Galerie für Zeitgenössische Kunst Leipzig, Leipzig 2002
Liverpool Biennial (group exh.), Liverpool, 2002
'The Volksboutique Style Manual' (solo exh.), Galerie Eigen & Art, Berlin, 2003

Select publications
Lost Paradise: Positionen der 90er Jahre, Oktagon, Stuttgart, 1995
Take me (I'm yours), Serpentine Gallery (exh. cat.), London, 1995
Nach Weimar, Cantz (exh. cat.), Ostfildern/Stuttgart, 1996
Volksboutique, Eigen & Art–Kunst-Werke Berlin (exh. cat.), Berlin, 1997
Talk. Show: die Kunst der Kommunikation in den 90er Jahren, Prestel (exh. cat.), Munich, 1999
Steiner, Barbara, *Inventory – Volksboutique and the work of Christine Hill*, Cantz, Ostfildern/Stuttgart, 2003

ILYA KABAKOV
b. 1933, Dnjepropetrovsk (Ukraine, former USSR); lives in New York (USA)

Select exhibitions
'Ilya Kabakov: The Untalented Artist and Other Characters' (solo exh.), ICA, London, 1989
'Documenta IX' (group exh.), Kassel, 1992
'The Boat of My Life' (solo exh.), Salzburger Kunstverein, Salzburg, 1993
'Ilya Kabakov: Installations 1983–1995' (solo exh.), Centre Georges Pompidou, Paris, 1995
'50 Installationen' (solo exh.), Kunstmuseum Bern, Bern, 2000

Select publications
Kabakov, Ilya, *Über die 'totale' Installation*, Cantz, Ostfildern/Stuttgart, 1995
Wallach, Amei, *Ilya Kabakov: The Man Who Never Threw Anything Away*, Harry N. Abrams Inc., New York, 1996
Ilya Kabakov: 1964–1983, Stimmen hinter der Tür, Galerie für Zeitgenössische Kunst Leipzig (exh. cat.), Leipzig, 1998
Zdenek, Felix (ed.), *Ilya Kabakov: Der Text als Grundlage des Visuellen*, Oktagon, Cologne, 1999
Kabakov, Ilya, *Ilya Kabakov die 60er und 70er Jahre: Aufzeichnungen über das inoffizielle Leben in Moskau*, Passagen-Verlag, Vienna, 2001

JOHANNA KANDL
b. 1954, Vienna (Austria); lives in Vienna (Austria)

Select exhibitions
'Johanna Kandl' (solo exh.), Secession, Vienna, 1999
'Johanna Kandl' (solo exh.), Galerie für Zeitgenössische Kunst Leipzig, Leipzig, 2002
'Touristische Blicke' (group exh.), Kunstverein Wolfsburg, 2002
'Uncommon Denominator: New Art from Vienna' (group exh.), Mass MOCA, North Adams, 2002
'B+B at home with Helmut und Johanna Kandl' (solo exh.), Galerie Christine König, Vienna, 2003

Select publications
Auf den Leib geschrieben, Kunsthalle Wien (exh. cat.), Vienna, 1995
Johanna Kandl, geschlossene Gesellschaft, Salzburger Kunstverein (exh. cat.), Salzburg, 1996
X squared: Kunst zwischen Arbeit und kollektiver Praxis, Secession (exh. cat.), Vienna, 1998
Ungemalt, Sammlung Essl (exh. cat.), Klosterneuburg, 2002
Johanna Kandl: Kämpfer fürs Glück, Kunstverein Ulm (exh. cat.), Ulm, 2003

ON KAWARA
b. 1933, Aichi (Japan); lives in New York (USA)

MARY KELLY
b. 1941, Fort Dodge (USA); lives in Los Angeles (USA)

Select exhibitions
'Interim' (solo exh.), The New Museum of Contemporary Art, New York, 1990
'Gloria Patri' (solo exh.), Institute of Contemporary Art, London, 1992
'Post-Partum Dokument: Das komplette Werk (1973–1979)' (solo exh.), Generali Foundation, Vienna, 1998
'Die verletzte Diva: Hysterie, Körper, Technik in der Kunst des 20. Jahrhunderts' (group exh.), Galerie im Taxispalais, Innsbruck, 2000
'Mea Culpa' (solo exh.), Robert Sandelson, London, 2001

Select publications
Lippard, Lucy R., *The Pink Glass Swan: Selected Feminist Essays on Art*, The New Press, New York, 1995
Kelly, Mary, *Imaging Desire*, MIT Press, Cambridge, Massachusetts, 1997
Graw, Isabelle, *Silberblick: Texte zu Kunst und Politik*, ID Verlag, Berlin, 1999

Kelly, Mary, *Rereading Post-Partum Document*, University of California Press (exh. cat.), Berkeley, California, 1999
Tate Modern: The Handbook, Tate Gallery (exh. cat.), London, 2000

WILLIAM KENTRIDGE
b. 1955, Johannesburg (South Africa); lives in Johannesburg (South Africa)

Select exhibitions
'Documenta X' (group exh.), Kassel, 1997
'William Kentridge' (solo exh.), Palais voor Schone Kunsten Brussels, Brussels, 1998
'William Kentridge' (solo exh.), Museum of Contemporary Art Chicago, Chicago, 2001
'Documenta XI' (group exh.), Kassel, 2002
'William Kentridge – Zeno Writing' (solo exh.), Marian Goodman Gallery, New York, 2002

Select publications
Enwezor, Okwui, *Truth and Responsibility: A Conversation with William Kentridge*, Parkett 54, New York, 1998
William Kentridge, Palais des Beaux-Arts de Bruxelles (exh. cat.), Brussels, 1998
Cameron, Dan (ed.), *William Kentridge*, Phaidon, London, 1999
Kentridge, William, *Weighting ... and Wanting*, Massachusetts Institute of Technology (exh. cat.), Cambridge, Massachusetts, 1999
Benezra, Neal (ed.), *William Kentridge*, Hirshhorn Museum (exh. cat.), Washington DC, 2001

JEFF KOONS
b. 1955, York, Pennsylvania (USA); lives in New York (USA)

Select exhibitions
'Banality' (solo exh.), Sonnabend Gallery, New York; Galerie Max Hetzler, Cologne; Donald Young Gallery, Chicago, Illinois, 1988
'Image World' (group exh.), Whitney Museum of American Art, New York, 1989
Sydney Biennial (group exh.), Sydney, 1990
Venice Biennale (group exh.), Venice, 1990
'Made in Heaven' (solo exh.), Sonnabend Gallery, New York, 1991
'Jeff Koons: Easyfun-Ethereal' (solo exh.), Deutsche Guggenheim Berlin, 2000; Guggenheim Museum Bilbao, Bilbao, 2001

Select publications
The Jeff Koons Handbook, Thames & Hudson, London, 1992

Muthesius, Angelika (ed.), *Jeff Koons*, Taschen, Cologne, 1992
Jeff Koons: A Millennium Celebration, Deste Foundation Center of Contemporary Art (exh. cat.), Athens, 1999
Jeff Koons: Easyfun-Ethereal, Guggenheim Museum Publications (exh. cat.), New York, 2000
Jeff Koons, Kunsthaus Bregenz (exh. cat.), Bregenz, 2001
Kellein, Thomas (ed.), *Jeff Koons: die Bilder 1980–2002*, Kunsthalle Bielefeld (exh. cat.), Bielefeld, 2002

ELKE KRYSTUFEK
b. 1970, Vienna (Austria); lives in Vienna (Austria)

Select exhibitions
'Protest & Survive' (group exh.), Whitechapel Art Gallery, London, 2000
'I am Your Man' (solo exh.), Ars Futura, Zurich, 2001
'He can't make babies, so he eats them' (solo exh.), Emily Tsingou Gallery, London, 2002
'Nackt & Mobil' (solo exh.), Sammlung Essl, Vienna, 2002
'Elke Krystufek' (solo exh.), Kunstraum Innsbruck, Innsbruck, 2003
'Selbst und Andere: das Bildnis in der Kunst nach 1960' (group exh.), Rupertinum, Salzburg, 2003
'Sex in the City' (group exh.), Kunsthalle Wien, Vienna, 2003

Select publications
I am Your Mirror, Secession Gallery (exh. cat.), Vienna, 1997
Elke Krystufek: Sleepingbetterland, Galerie Georg Kargl (exh. cat.), Vienna, 1999
Krystufek, Elke, *In the arms of luck*, Centre Genevois de Gravure Contemporain (exh. cat.), Geneva, 1999
ELKE KRYSTUFEK NOBODY HAS TO KNOW, Galerie Georg Kargl (exh. cat.), Vienna, 2000
Alms, Barbara (ed.), *Wirklichkeit in der Zeitgenössischen Kunst*, Hauschild, Bremen, 2001

FRIEDL KUBELKA
b. 1946, London (UK); lives in Vienna (Austria) and London (UK)

Select exhibitions
'Fotoarchiv' (solo exh.), Center of Contemporary Art, Warsaw, 1990
'Identität: Differenz' (group exh.), Steierischer Herbst, Graz, 1996

'Portrait of Louise Anna Kubelka' (solo exh.), Galerie Fotohof, Salzburg, 1998
'Friedl Kubelka: Fotografie und Malerei' (solo exh.), Kunsthaus der Stadt Graz, Graz, 1999
'Sammlung' (group exh.), Generali Foundation, Vienna, 2003

Select publications
Elf Ausschnitte aus dem Dritten Jahresportrait 1982–1983, Museum Moderner Kunst (exh. cat.), Vienna, 1984
Kubelka, Friedl, *Schaulust: Schule für künstlerische Photographie*, Edition Camera Austria, Graz, 1998
Rupertinum Fotopreis 1997, Österreichischen Fotogalerie (exh. cat.), Salzburg, 1998
Breitwieser, Sabine (ed.), *Double Life: Identität und Transformation in der Zeitgenössischen Kunst*, Generali Foundation (exh. cat.), Vienna, 2001

ANITA LEISZ
b. 1973, Leoben (Austria); lives in Vienna (Austria)

Select exhibitions
'Time Out' (group exh.), Kunsthalle Nürnberg, Nuremberg, 1997
'x-squared' (group exh.), Secession Gallery, Vienna, 1997
'Die letzten Ereignisse' (solo exh.), Kunstverein Ludwigsburg, Ludwigsburg, 1998
'Studio City 2' (group exh.), Kunstverein Wolfsburg, Wolfsburg, 1999
'Anita Leisz: Rauminstallation' (solo exh.), Galerie Krobath & Wimmer, Vienna, 2000

Select publications
Stange, Raimar, *Der Comicmensch: Zu den narrativen Eingriffen von Anita Leisz*, Kunstbulletin, Zurich, 1998
Steiner, Barbara (ed.), *Den Rest: die letzten Ereignisse*, Kunstverein Ludwigsburg (exh. cat.), Ludwigsburg, 1998
Anita Leisz, Secession Gallery (exh. cat.), Vienna, 2000
Spiegl, Andreas, *Dramaturgie des Alltäglichen*, Artist Kunstmagazin, Bremen, 2000

WIEBKE LOEPER
b. 1972, Berlin (Germany); lives in Berlin (Germany)

Select exhibitions
'Sanseveria' (solo exh.), Galerie Wohnmaschine, Berlin, 1992

'Portrait Berlin' (group exh.), Plaza Gallery Tokyo, Tokyo, 2001
'Hello from Bloomer: Viele Grüße aus Wismar', (solo exh.), Raum-Zeitgenössische Kunst in der Philosophie, Wismar, 2002
'5th Africa Photography Encounters Bamako', (group exh.), Mali, 2003
'Öffentlich – Privat' (group exh.), Galerie für Zeitgenössische Kunst Leipzig, Leipzig, 2003

Select publications
Loeper, Wiebke, *MOLL 31*, Edition Liane, Berlin, 1995
Loeper, Wiebke, *Gold und Silber lieb ich sehr*, Edition S.E.E.O., Berlin, 1998
Lad, Goldrausch Künstlerinnenprojekt, Künstlerhaus Bethanien (exh. cat.), Berlin, 2001
Loeper, Wiebke, *Hello from Bloomer: Viele Grüße aus Wismar*, Edition J. J. Heckenhauer, Tübingen, 2001

DORIT MARGREITER
b. 1967, Vienna (Austria); lives in Vienna (Austria)

Select exhibitions
'Short Hills' (solo exh.), Grazer Kunstverein, Graz, 1999
'Studio City' (group exh.), IPZ, Vienna, and Kunstverein Wolfsburg, Wolfsburg, 1999
'Dorit Margreiter: Everyday Life' (solo exh.), Galerie am Taxispalais, Innsbruck, 2001
'Event Horizon' (solo exh.), Galerie Krobath Wimmer, Vienna, 2002
'Routes: Imaging Travel and Migration' (solo exh.), Grazer Kunstverein, Graz, 2002

Select publications
Die Arena des Privaten, Kunstverein München (exh. cat.), Munich, 1993
Hers: video as a female terrain, Springer-Verlag (exh. cat.), Vienna, 2000
Eiblmayr, Silvia (ed.), *Dorit Margreiter: Everyday Life*, Triton (exh. cat.), Vienna, 2001
Kravagna, Christian (ed.), *Das Museum als Arena: Institutionskritische Texte von KünstlerInnen*, Walther König, Cologne, 2001
Stadler, Eva (ed.), *Dorit Margreiter: Short Hills*, Grazer Kunstverein (exh. cat.), Graz, 2002

OLIVER MUSOVIK
b. 1971, Skopje (Macedonia); lives in Skopje (Macedonia)

Select exhibitions
'Neighbours 2: The Yard' (group exh.), Museum of Contemporary Art, Skopje, 1999
'Schuhe ausziehen' (solo exh.), CIX-Galerie, Skopje, 1999
6th International Istanbul Biennale (group exh.), Istanbul, 1999
'In den Schluchten des Balkan' (group exh.), Kunsthalle Fridericianum, Kassel, 2003
'Introducing Sites' (group exh.), Galerie für Zeitgenössische Kunst Leipzig, 2003

Select publications
Dimitrov, Valentino, 'Everyday Everyday Everyday Everyday and Ends', in, *The Large Glass*, Skopje, 2000
Part of the System, Rotor: Association for Contemporary Art (exh. cat.), Graz, 2000
Korrespondenzen, IFA-Galerie (exh. cat.), Berlin, 2001
Sunny Moon: Month of Contemporary Art, Museum of Contemporary Art (exh. cat.), Zagreb, 2001
Oliver Musovik – Neighbours 2: The Yard, Museum of Contemporary Art (exh. cat.), Skopje, 2002

ANNY ÖZTÜRK
b. 1970, Istanbul (Turkey); lives in Offenbach (Germany)

SIBEL ÖZTÜRK
b. 1975, Eberbach/Neckar (Germany); lives in Offenbach (Germany)

Select exhibitions
'Anny Öztürk: 19' (solo exh.), Galerie Anita Beckers, Frankfurt am Main, 1999
'I love you too, but… – Positionen zwischen Comic-Ästhetik und Narration' (group exh.), Galerie für Zeitgenössische Kunst Leipzig, Leipzig, 2000
'Germania' (group exh.), Palazzo delle Papesse, Siena, 2001
'Heimaten' (group exh.), Galerie für Zeitgenössische Kunst Leipzig, Leipzig, 2001
'Muster Frau' (group exh.), Kunsthalle Darmstadt, Darmstadt, 2002
'Touristische Blicke' (group exh.), Kunstverein Wolfsburg, Wolfsburg, 2002

Select publications
Evelyn, 1822 Forum (exh. cat.), Frankfurt, 2000
Dogramaci, Burcu, *Die dritte Generation*, Art, Hamburg, 2001
Germinations 13: Get Out! An Exhibition on the Subject of Going Away, Allianz Kulturstiftung (exh. cat.), Munich, 2001

Grammel, Sören (ed.), *Get Out! An Exhibition on the Subject of Going Away*, Galeria Arsenal (exh. cat.), Bialystock, 2002
Steiner, Barbara, 'Cultural Territories: A New Concept of Nation', *Flash Art* No. 224, Milan, 2002

RIA PACQUÉE
b. 1954, Merksem (Belgium); lives in Antwerp (Belgium)

Select exhibitions
'Oh boy, it's a girl' (group exh.), Kunstverein München, Munich, 1994
'Masque' (group exh.), John Hansard Gallery, University of Southampton, Southampton, 1998
'Story Telling' (group exh.), Casino Luxembourg, Luxembourg, 1999
'Desert of Fragments' (solo exh.), Museum van Hedendaagse Kunst, Antwerp, 2001
'Humanism II' (group exh.), Orion Art Gallery Brussels/Ostend, Ostend, 2002

Select publications
Engblom, Sören (ed.), *Rum Mellan Rum*, Moderna Museet (exh. cat.), Stockholm, 1992
Ria Pacquée, Provinciaal Museum Hasselt (exh. cat.), Hasselt, 1995
Foncé, Jan & Maaretta Jaukkuri (eds), *Above–below the surface*, Museum van Hedendaagse Kunst (exh. cat.), Antwerp, 1996
Dewachter, Lillian (ed.), *Ria Pacquée: Desert of Fragments*, Museum van Hedendaagse, Antwerp (exh. cat.), 2001
Breitwieser, Sabine (ed.), *Double Life: Identität und Transformation in der Zeitgenössischen Kunst*, Generali Foundation (exh. cat.), Vienna, 2001

ADRIAN PIPER
b. 1948, New York (USA); lives in Cape Cod, Massachusetts (USA)

Select exhibitions
'Adrian Piper: A Retrospective' (solo exh.), New Museum of Contemporary Art, New York, 2001
'Antagonismes: Casos d'estudi' (group exh.), Museu d'Art Contemporani de Barcelona, Barcelona, 2001
'Adrian Piper' (solo exh.), Galleria Emi Fontana, Milan, 2002
'Adrian Piper seit 1965: Metakunst und Kunstkritik' (solo exh.), Generali Foundation, Vienna, 2002
'Documenta 11' (group exh.), Kassel, 2002

Select publications
Piper, Adrian, *Colored People*, Book Works, London, 1991
Golden, Thelma, *Black Male: Representations of Masculinity in Contemporary American Art*, Whitney Museum of American Art (exh. cat.), New York, 1994
Piper, Adrian, *Out of Order, Out of Sight*, MIT Press, Cambridge, Massachusetts, 1996
'Conceptual Art and Feminism', *Woman's Art Journal*, 2001
Walking in the City, Kunsthalle Fridericianum (exh. cat.), Kassel, 2003

RASSIM® (Казаimir KRASTEV)
b. 1972, Pleven (Bulgaria); lives in Sofia (Bulgaria)

Select exhibitions
'Corrections' (group exh.), Fonds Régional d'Art Contemporain, Montpellier, 1999
'Inventing a People: Contemporary Art in the Balkans' (group exh.), National Gallery for Foreign Art, Sofia, 1999
'After the Wall' (group exh.), Hamburger Bahnhof, Berlin, 2000
'Body and the East' (group exh.), EXIT ART, New York, 2001
'Capital & Gender' (group exh.), Contemporary Arts Center, Skopje, 2001

Select publications
Body and the East, Museum of Modern Art (exh. cat.), Ljubljana, 1998
Bulgariaavantgarde, Salon-Verlag (exh. cat.), Cologne, 1998
Made in Bulgaria, Art as Natie, CCA Sofia (exh. cat.), Sofia, 1999
Made in Bulgaria, Center of Contemporary Art (exh. cat.), Sofia, 1999
After the Wall, Hamburger Bahnhof (exh. cat.), Berlin, 2000

GERHARD RICHTER
b. 1932, Dresden (Germany); lives in Berlin (Germany)

Select exhibitions
'Gerhard Richter' (solo exh.), Städtische Galerie München, Munich, 1973
'Atlas' (solo exh.), Museum Ludwig, Cologne,1990
'Documenta 10' (group exh.), Kassel, 1997
'Gerhard Richter: Bilder 1996–2001' (solo exh.), Marian Goodman Gallery, New York, 2001
'Gerhard Richter' (solo exh.), Museum of Modern Art, New York, 2002

Select publications
Gerhard Richter 1988–89, Museum Boymans-Van Beuningen (exh. cat.), Rotterdam, 1989
Gerhard Richter, Tate Gallery London (exh. cat.), London, 1991
Gerhard Richter: Werkübersicht/Catalogue raisonné, Cantz, Ostfildern/Stuttgart, 1993
Henatsch, Martin, *Gerhard Richter: 18 Oktober 1977, das verwischte Bild der Geschichte*, Fischer, Frankfurt am Main, 1998
Gerhard Richter: Forty Years of Painting, Museum of Modern Art (exh. cat.), San Francisco, California, 2003

TRACEY ROSE
b. 1974, Durban (South Africa); lives in Johannesburg (South Africa)

Select exhibitions
'South Meets West' (group exh.), National Museum of Ghana, 1999
'Videodrome' (group exh.), The New Museum of Contemporary Art, New York, 1999
'Cross + Over' (group exh.), CPC Path Studios, Johannesburg, 2000
'DAK'Art' (group exh.), Dakar Biennale, Dakar, Senegal, 2000
'Ciao Bella' (solo exh.), The Goodman Gallery, Johannesburg, 2002

Select publications
7. Triennale der Kleinplastik, 1998: Zeitgenössische Skulptur Afrika, Cantz (exh. cat.), Ostfildern/Stuttgart, 1998
Guarene Arte 98, Fondazione Sandretto Re Rebaudengo per l'Arte (exh. cat.), Guarene, 1998
Video cult/ures: multimediale Installationen der 90er Jahre, DuMont (exh. cat.), Cologne, 1999
In the mean time..., De Appel (exh. cat.), Amsterdam, 2001
The Hope I Hope: Faces of Truth, Ayloul Festival (exh. cat.), Beirut, 2001

ANRI SALA
b. 1974, Tirana (Albania); lives in Paris (France)

Select exhibitions
'Manifesta 3' (group exh.), Ljubljana, 2000
'Anri Sala: It has been raining here' (solo exh.), Galerie Chantal Crousel, Paris, 2001
Venice Biennale (group exh.), Venice, 2001
'Anri Sala: Amplified Absorbers' (solo exh.), Galerie Hauser & Wirth, Zurich, 2002
'Anri Sala' (solo exh.), Kunsthalle Wien, Vienna, 2003

Select publications
Anri Sala, De Appel (exh. cat.), Amsterdam, 2000
The Hugo Prize 2002, Guggenheim Museum (exh. cat.), New York, 2002
Le Prix Marcel Duchamp 2002, Centre National d'Art et de Culture Georges Pompidou (exh. cat.), Paris, 2002
Dziewior, Yilmaz & Karola Grässlin (eds), *Zusammenhänge herstellen*, Du Mont (exh. cat.), Cologne, 2003
Sala, Anri, *A Thousand Windows*, Walther König, Cologne, 2003

ANTJE SCHIFFERS
b. 1967, Wolfsburg (Germany); lives in Berlin (Germany)

Select exhibitions
'Da wo ich war' (solo exh.), Galerie Konstantin Adamopoulos, Frankfurt am Main, 2000
'Germania' (group exh.), Palazzo delle Papesse, Siena, 2001
'Bin in der Steppe' (solo exh.), Kunstverein Wolfsburg, Wolfsburg, 2002
'Perspektiven' (group exh.), Kunstverein Hannover, Hannover, 2002
're-orientation' (group exh.), ACC-Galerie Weimar, Weimar, 2002

Select publications
Schiffers, Antje, *Bin in der Steppe*, Revolver, Frankfurt am Main, 2003

SHIRANA SHAHBAZI
b. 1974, Tehran (Iran); lives in Zurich (Switzerland)

Select exhibitions
'Heimaten' (group exh.), Galerie für Zeitgenössische Kunst Leipzig, Leipzig, 2001
'Shirana Shahbazi' (solo exh.), Kunstverein Freiburg, Freiburg im Breisgau, 2001
'Shirana Shahbazi: New Work' (solo exh.), Galerie Bob van Orsouw, Zurich, 2002
'Shirana Shahbazi: Goftare Nik (Good Words)' (solo exh.), The Museum of Contemporary Photography, Chicago, Illinois, 2003
Venice Biennale (group exh.), Venice, 2003

Select publications
Ruf, Beatrix (ed.), *Shirana Shahbazi: Goftare Nik (Good Words)*, Codax Publisher (exh. cat.), Zurich, 2001
Shahbazi, Shirana, *Shahrzad*, Kunsthalle Zürich (exh. cat.), Zurich, 2002

Shirana Shahbazi, Bonner Kunstverein (exh. cat.), Bonn, 2002
'Ethnic Marketing', *Material,* Migros Museum, Zurich, 2003

CINDY SHERMAN
b. 1954, New Jersey (USA); lives in New York (USA)

Select exhibitions
'Documenta 7' (group exh.), Kassel, 1982
Cindy Sherman (solo exh.), Whitney Museum of American Art, New York, 1987
'Cindy Sherman Retrospective' (solo exh.), Museum of Modern Art, Shiga, 1996; Museum of Contemporary Art, Los Angeles, 1997; Museum of Contemporary Art, Sydney, 1999
'Veronica's Revenge' (group exh.), Museum of Contemporary Art, Sydney, 2001
'Cindy Sherman', Serpentine Gallery, London, 2003

Select publications
Krauss, Rosalind, *Cindy Sherman: 1975–1993,* Rizzoli, New York, 1993
Neven Du Mont, Gisela & Wilfried Dickhoff (eds), *Cindy Sherman,* DuMont, Cologne, 1995
Gothic: Transmutations of Horror in Late Twentieth Century Art, Institute of Contemporary Art (exh. cat.), Boston, Massachusetts, 1997
Beudert, Monique & Sean Rainbird (eds), *Contemporary Art: The Janet Wolfson De Botton Gift,* Tate Gallery Publishing (exh. cat.), London, 1998
Cindy Sherman: Untitled Film Stills, Schirmer-Mosel, Munich, 1998
Sherman, Cindy, *Early Work of Cindy Sherman,* Glenn Horowitz Bookseller, New York, 2000
Wiehager, Renate (ed.), *Moving Pictures,* Cantz (exh. cat.), Ostfildern/Stuttgart, 2001

RUBY SIRCAR
b. 1975, Bietigheim (Germany); lives in Stuttgart (Germany) and London (UK)

Select exhibitions
'@mp asiatic mode of production' (solo exh.), Akademie der bildenden Künste, Vienna, 2000
'Screenings' (solo exh.), Künstlerhaus Stuttgart, Stuttgart, 2000
'Heimaten' (group exh.), Galerie für Zeitgenössische Kunst Leipzig, Leipzig, 2001
'Race in the Digital Space 2.0' (solo exh.), University of Southern California, Los Angeles, 2002

Select publications
'Try and get me', in, *Expressgut,* Staatliche Akademie der Bildenden Künste Stuttgart, Stuttgart, 1999
'@mp' and 'Screening', in, *Exhibitionzine,* Künstlerhaus Stuttgart, Stuttgart, 2000
'@mp', in, *Medien in den Medien,* Cologne University/DuMont, Cologne, 2002
'An Exhibition, Indian Exoticism and Art Must-Mast: Essays for Diaspora', *online-zine,* theinder.ne, 2002

RIRKRIT TIRAVANIJA
b. 1961, Buenos Aires (Argentina); lives in Thailand and Berlin (Germany)

Select exhibitions
'Untitled 1996' (solo exh.), Kölnischer Kunstverein, Cologne, 1996
'Rirkrit Tiravanija' (solo exh.), Villa Franck, Kunstverein Ludwigsburg, Ludwigsburg, 1997
'Untitled, 1998 (Das soziale Kapital)' (solo exh.), Migros Museum, Museum für Gegenwartskunst, Zurich, 1998
'Untitled 1999 (reading from right to left)' (solo exh.), Wexner Center for the Arts, Columbus, Ohio, 1999
'Rikrit Tiravanija: Untitled 2001 (No Fire No Ashes)' (solo exh.), Neugerriemschneider, Berlin, 2001

Select publications
Kittelmann, Udo (ed.), *Rirkrit Tiravanija: Untitled 1996 (tomorrow is another day),* Kölnischer Kunstverein (exh. cat.), Cologne, 1997
Steiner, Barbara, *Rirkrit Tiravanija: Kochbuch,* Kunstverein Ludwigsburg, Ludwigsburg, 1997
Supermarket, Migros Museum, Museum für Gegenwartskunst (exh. cat.), Zurich, 1998
Möntmann, Nina, *Kunst als sozialer Raum,* Walther König, Cologne, 2002
Rirkrit Tiravanija: Secession, 5 July–1 September 2002, Walther König (exh. cat.), Cologne, 2003

TOBIAS Z. (Gert and Uwe TOBIAS)
b. 1973, Neustadt/Siebenbürgen (Romania); live in Cologne (Germany)

Select exhibitions
'Lebenszeichen' (group exh.), Kunstverladehalle, Rüsselsheim, 1997
'MAKE MY PAPER SOUND' (group exh.), Kunstverein Braunschweig, Braunschweig, 2000
'Germania' (group exh.), Palazzo delle Papesse, Siena, 2001
'Heimaten' (group exh.), Galerie für Zeitgenössische Kunst Leipzig, Leipzig, 2001

'Internationale Gruppenausstellung' (group exh.), Appartments der Kunststiftung Baden-Württemberg, Stuttgart, 2001
'Projekt der HBK Braunschweig' (group exh.), Städtische Galerie Wolfsburg, Wolfsburg, 2002
'Projektreihe: WOCHENEND' (group exh.), Schnitt Ausstellungsraum, Cologne, 2003

Select publications
Le Repubbliche dell'arte: Germania, la costruzione di un'immagine, Palazzo delle Papesse (exh. cat.), Siena, 2001
Schultze, Arved & Steffi Wurster, *X-Wohnungen,* Alexander Verlag, Berlin, 2003

ROSEMARIE TROCKEL
b. 1952, Schwerte (Germany); lives in Cologne (Germany)

Select exhibitions
Venice Biennale (group exh.), Venice, 1999
'Rosemarie Trockel: Metamorphoses and Mutations' (solo exh.), Centre National d'Art et de Culture Georges Pompidou, Paris, 2000
'Rosemarie Trockel' (solo exh.), Moderna Museet, Stockholm, 2001
'Rosemarie Trockel: Das Kinderzimmer im MMK' (solo exh.), Museum für Moderne Kunst, Frankfurt am Main, 2003
'Rosemarie Trockel: Retrospective' (solo exh.), Tallinna Kunstihoone, Tallinn, 2003

Select publications
Laue, Monika, 'Wahre Weibeskünste? Zur Problematik einer femininen Ästhetik in der zeitgenössischen Kunst: Cindy Sherman, Rosemarie Trockel, und Rebecca Horn', in, *Punktum,* scaneg cop, Munich, 1996
Rosemarie Trockel: Bodies of Work 1986–1998, Whitechapel Art Gallery (exh. cat.), London, 1998
Friedel, Helmut (ed.), *Rosemarie Trockel: Skulpturen, Videos, Zeichnungen,* Wienand, Cologne, 2000
Bethenod, Martin, *Rosemarie Trockel: Dessins,* Centre Georges Pompidou (exh. cat.), Paris, 2001
Goetz, Ingvild (ed.), *Rosemarie Trockel, Sammlung Goetz* (exh. cat.), Munich, 2002

ANDY WARHOL
b. 1928, Pittsburgh (USA); d. 1987, New York (USA)

Select exhibitions
'The Warhol Look: Glamour, Style, Fashion' (solo exh.), Whitney Museum of American Art, New York, 1997

'Andy Warhol: Shadows' (solo exh.), Dia Center for the Arts, New York, 1998
'Andy Warhol: Photography' (solo exh.), Hamburger Kunsthalle, Hamburg, 1999
'Andy Warhol and his World' (solo exh.), Louisiana Museum of Modern Art, Humlebaek, 2000

Select publications
Andy Warhol: A Retrospective, Museum of Modern Art (exh. cat.), New York, 1989
Sabin, Stefana, *Andy Warhol: Mit Selbstzeugnissen und Bilddokumenten,* Rowohlt, Hamburg, 1992
O'Conner, John (ed.), *Unseen Warhol*, Rizzoli, New York, 1996
About face: Andy Warhol portraits, Wadsworth Atheneum (exh. cat.), Hartford, Connecticut, 2000
Bastian, Heiner (ed.), *Andy Warhol: Retrospektive,* DuMont, Cologne, 2001

JOHANNES WOHNSEIFER
b. 1967, Cologne (Germany); lives in Cologne (Germany)

Select exhibitions
'Der Stadtstreicher' (solo exh.), Galerie Gisela Capitain, Cologne, 1998
'Projektraum: Johannes Wohnseifer' (solo exh.), Museum Ludwig, Cologne, 1999
'I'm beginning to see the light' (solo exh.), Neues Museum für Kunst und Design, Nuremberg, 2002
'Into the Light' (solo exh.), Ludwig Forum für Internationale Kunst, Aachen, 2003
'Johannes Wohnseifer – Leere und Gewalt 1978–2003 – Interventionen 31' (solo exh.), Sprengel Museum Hannover, Hannover, 2003

Select publications
Ausstellung Monika Baer – Johannes Wohnseifer, Bonner Kunstverein (exh. cat.), Bonn, 1998
El Nino, Städtisches Museum Abteiberg (exh. cat.), Mönchengladbach, 1998
German Open: Gegenwartskunst in Deutschland, Cantz (exh. cat.), Ostfildern/ Stuttgart, 1999
Kunst nach Kunst, Hauschild (exh. cat.), Bremen, 2002

JUN YANG
b. 1975, Qingtian (China); lives in Vienna (Austria)

Select exhibitions
'Jun Yang' (solo exh.), Kunstverein Wolfsburg, Wolfsburg, 2000; Galerie für Zeitgenössische Kunst, Leipzig, 2001

'Heimaten' (group exh.), Galerie für Zeitgenössische Kunst Leipzig, Leipzig, 2001
'In the mean time...', De Appel (group exh.), Amsterdam, 2001
'Manifesta 4' (group exh.), Frankfurt, 2002
'Jun Yang', Galerie Martin Janda (solo exh.), Vienna, 2003

Select publications
Spiegl, Andreas, 'I-like a Ceremony', *Eikon* No. 29, Vienna, 1999
Jun Yang: Reconstruction: coming home – daily structures of life, Museum für angewandte Kunst (exh. cat.), Vienna, 2001
Tasch, S., 'Phönix aus der Reisetasche', *TAZ* 23.4.01, Berlin, 2001
Rebhandl, Bert, 'Man of the world: Bert Rebhandl on Jun Yang', *frieze* No. 73, 2003
Vogel, Sabine B., 'Look like them talk like them', *Kunst Bulletin* No. 1, Zurich, 2003

MOIRA ZOITL
b. 1968, Salzburg (Austria); lives in Berlin (Germany)

Select exhibitions
'jobs routine bauten' (solo exh.), Atelier Wilhelmstrasse, Stuttgart, 2001
'ORTung 2000' (group exh.), Galerie 5020, Salzburg, 2001
'Urban Nomads' (group exh.), South London Gallery, London, 2001
'Talk of the Town' (group exh.), Kunstraum München, Munich, 2002
'Thema: Frauen: Thema: I: Alltag' (group exh.), Fotogalerie Wien, Vienna, 2002

Select publications
Zoitl, Moira, *chicago research*, Künstlerhaus Wien (exh. cat.), Vienna, 1998
Printed Matter 1–9, Museumsquartier Wien (exh. cat.), Vienna, 2000
Traversals, Map Book Publishers, Hong Kong, 2001
Thema: Frauen: Thema, Fotogalerie Wien (exh. cat.), Vienna, 2002

FURTHER READING

Ashley, Kathleen, Leigh Gilmore and Gerald Peters (eds), *Autobiography & Postmodernism*, Amherst, 1994

Barthes, Roland, *Roland Barthes par Roland Barthes*, Paris, 1975

Bell, Susan Groag, and Marilyn Yalom (eds), *Revealing Lives: Autobiography, Biography, and Gender*, New York, 1990

Brinthaupt, Thomas M., and Richard P. Lipka (eds), *Changing the Self: Philosophies, Techniques, and Experiences*, Albany, 1994

Eakin, Paul John, *Fictions in Autobiography: Studies in the Art of Self Invention*, Princeton, 1985

–, *How Our Lives Become Stories: Making Selves*, Ithaca and London, 1999

Egan, Susanna, *Patterns of Experience in Autobiography*, Chapel Hill and London, 1984

Elbaz, Robert, *The Changing Nature of the Self: A Critical Study of the Autobiographic Discourse*, London, 1988

Foucault, Michel, *Discipline and Punish: The Birth of the Prison* (1976), London, 1977

–, *Madness and Civilization: A History of Insanity in the Age of Reason* (1961), London, 1967

Freud, Sigmund, *The Standard Edition of the Complete Psychological Works of Sigmund Freud*, ed. James Strachey, London, 1953

Gilmore, Leigh, *The Limits of Autobiography: Trauma and Testimony*, Ithaca and London, 2001

Goodman, Katherine R., *Dis/closures: Women's Autobiography in Germany between 1790 and 1914*, New York, 1986

Goodman, Kay, 'Die große Kunst nach innen zu weinen: Autobiographien deutscher Frauen im späten 19. und frühen 20. Jahrhundert', in: Wolfgang Paulsen, *Die Frau als Heldin und Autorin*, Bern & Munich, 1979

–, 'Weibliche Autobiographien', in: Hiltrud Gnüg and Renate Möhrmann (eds), *Frauen Literatur Geschichte*, Stuttgart, 1985

Haverty Rugg, Linda, *Picturing Ourselves: Photography and Autobiography*, Chicago and London, 1997

Heuser, Magdalene, *Autobiographien von Frauen: Beiträge zu ihrer Geschichte*, Tübingen, 1996

Jung, Carl, *Memories, Dreams, Reflections*, ed. Aniela Jaffé, trans. Richard and Clara Winston, London, 1967

Lacan, Jacques, 'The Mirror Stage as Formative of the Function of the I as Revealed in Psychoanalytic Theory' (1949), in: *Ecrits: A Selection*, trans. Alan Sheridan, London, 1977

–, 'The Subject and the Other: Alienation', in: Jacques-Alain Miller (ed.), *The Four Fundamental Concepts of Psycho-analysis* (1964), trans. Alan Sheridan, Harmondsworth, 1979

–, 'What is a Picture?', in: Jacques-Alain Miller (ed.), *The Four Fundamental Concepts of Psycho-analysis* (1964), trans. Alan Sheridan, Harmondsworth, 1979

Lejeune, Philippe, *Le pacte autobiographique*, Paris, 1975

Monsman, Gerald, *Walter Pater's Art of Autobiography*, New Haven and London, 1980

Okely, Judith, and Helen Callaway (eds), *Anthropology and Autobiography*, London and New York, 1992

Olney, James (ed.), *Autobiography: Essays Theoretical and Critical*, Princeton, 1980

Proust, Marcel, *Remembrance of Things Past*, trans. C. K. Scott Moncrieff, Terence Kilmartin and Andreas Mayor, London, 1981

Reed-Danahay, Deborah (ed.), *Auto/ethnography: Rewriting the Self and the Social*, Oxford, 1997

Rousseau, Jean-Jacques, *Confessions*, ed. Patrick Coleman, trans. Angela Scholar, Oxford, 2000

Sagarra, Eda, 'Quellenbibliographie autobiographischer Schriften von Frauen im deutschen Kulturraum 1730–1918', in, *IASL*, Jg. 11, 1986

St Augustine, *Confessions*, Oxford, 1992

Smith, Robert, *Derrida and Autobiography*, Cambridge, 1995

Smith, Sidonie, *Subjectivity, Identity and the Body: Women's Autobiographical Practice in the 20th Century*, Bloomington, 1993

–, and Julia Watson (eds), *Getting a Life: Everyday Uses of Autobiography*, Minneapolis, 1996

– (eds), *Women, Autobiography, Theory: A Reader*, Madison and London, 1998

Stanton, Domna, *The Female Autograph: Theory and Practice of Autobiography from the Tenth to the Twentieth Century*, Chicago and London, 1987

Ugrešic, Dubravka, *The Museum of Unconditional Surrender* (1996), New York, 1999

Weintraub, Karl Joachim, *The Value of the Individual: Self and Circumstance in Autobiography*, Chicago and London, 1978

ILLUSTRATION LIST

Measurements are given in centimetres, followed by inches, height before width before depth.

1 Tracey Emin, *My Bed*, 1998. Installation view. Mattress, linens, pillows, rope, various memorabilia, 79 x 211 x 234 (31 x 83 x 92). © The artist. Courtesy Jay Jopling/White Cube (London). Photo Stephen White

2 Elke Krystufek, *Your Daddy*, 2001 (detail). Acrylic on canvas, 70 x 50 (27 1/2 x 19 5/8). Private collection. Courtesy GEORG KARGL Fine Arts, Vienna

3 Eleanor Antin, *The Angel of Mercy*, 1976–77 (detail). Black and white photograph, 21.3 x 13.3 (8 3/8 x 5 1/4). Collection Whitney Museum of American Art, New York

4–5 Shirana Shahbazi, *Goftare Nik/Good Words*, 2000–2. Installation view: GFZK Leipzig Courtesy the artist and Galerie Bob van Orsouw, Zurich. Photo H.-Ch. Schink

6 Anny and Sibel Öztürk, *Re-Collection (Frankfurter Zimmer)*, 2000. Installation view. Courtesy the artists

10 Jun Yang, *Waverly*, 2002. Colour photograph, dimensions variable. Courtesy the artist

14 Lynn Hershman, *Roberta*, 1976. Colour photograph, 116.8 x 88.9 (46 x 35). Courtesy the artist and Gallery Paule Anglim, San Francisco

17 Elke Krystufek, *A territory to be mastered in the same as patagonia*, 2001. Installation view. Silk and plastic plant, c-prints, dimensions variable. Courtesy the artist and GEORG KARGL Fine Arts, Vienna

18 Sophie Calle (with Greg Shephard), *Double Blind (No Sex Last Night)*, 1992. Video still. Courtesy the artist and Emmanuel Perrotin. © ADAGP, Paris and DACS, London 2004

23 (above) Shirana Shahbazi, [Dokhtar-07-2002], from *Goftare Nik/Good Words*, 2000–2. Colour photograph. Courtesy the artist and Galerie Bob van Orsouw, Zurich

23 (below) Shirana Shahbazi, [Tehran-09-2002], from *Goftare Nik/Good Words*, 2000–2. Colour photograph. Courtesy the artist and Galerie Bob van Orsouw, Zurich

24 (above and below) William Kentridge, *Johannesburg, Second Greatest City after Paris*, 1989. Charcoal drawings, 105 x 20 (41 3/8 x 7 7/8). Courtesy the artist

25 Johanna Kandl, *o.T. (Tea and Coffee...)*, 1999. Tempera on wood, 59 x 80 (23 1/4 x 31 1/2). Photo H. & J. Kandl. Courtesy Galerie Christine König, Vienna, and Firma KAPO, Pöllau

30 (above) Lynn Hershman, *Roberta meets I*, 1976. Colour photograph, 116.8 x 88.9 (46 x 35). Courtesy the artist and Gallery Paule Anglim, San Francisco

30 (below) Lynn Hershman, *Multiples*, 1976. Colour photograph, 50.8 x 40.6 (20 x 16). Courtesy the artist and Gallery Paule Anglim, San Francisco

31 Lynn Hershman, *Psychiatric Sessions*, 1976. Black and white photograph, 83.8 x 58.4 (33 x 23). Courtesy the artist and Gallery Paule Anglim, San Francisco

32 Lynn Hershman, *The Electronic Diaries*, 1984. Digital print collage, 20.3 x 25.4 (8 x 10). Courtesy the artist and Gallery Paule Anglim, San Francisco

33 Lynn Hershman, *The Electronic Diaries: First Person Plural*, 1984. Black and white photograph, 20.3 x 25.4 (8 x 10). Courtesy the artist and Gallery Paule Anglim, San Francisco

34 Eleanor Antin, *The King*, 1973. Black and white photograph, 23 x 15.5 (9 x 6). Courtesy Ronald Feldman Fine Arts, New York

35 Eleanor Antin, *The Ballerina*, 1974. Black and white photograph, 24.2 x 17.7 (9 1/2 x 7). Courtesy Ronald Feldman Fine Arts, New York

36 Eleanor Antin, *The Nurse*, 1976. Black and white photograph, 24.6 x 16.7 (9 5/8 x 6 5/8). Courtesy Ronald Feldman Fine Arts, New York

37 Eleanor Antin, *The Angel of Mercy*, 1976–77. Black and white photograph, 21.3 x 13.3 (8 3/8 x 5 1/4). Collection Whitney Museum of American Art, New York

38 (above and below) Anita Leisz, *Den Rest*, 1998. Plotted drawings, dimensions variable. Courtesy the artist

39–43 Anita Leisz, *Are those your relatives?*, 2002. Text and photocollage. Courtesy the artist

44 (above) Oliver Hangl, *Children* (from the series 'Picture This!'), 2001. Digital montage from stereo photographs, 50 x 50 (19 5/8 x 19 5/8). Courtesy the artist

44 (below) Oliver Hangl, *Lucky like Daniel Rose*, 1997. Paper collage/exhibition poster, 15 x 10 (5 7/8 x 3 7/8). Courtesy the artist

45 (top left) Oliver Hangl, *Daniel Rose: shooting exercise*, 1990. Photograph, 50 x 70 (19 5/8 x 27 1/2). Courtesy the artist

45 (top centre and top right) Oliver Hangl, *two timing 2*, 2002. Stereo photographs, 122 x 59.5 (48 x 23 3/8). Courtesy the artist

45 (middle row, centre) Oliver Hangl, *Mr Rose*, 2000. Audio CD. Courtesy the artist

45 (middle row, right) Georg Wagenhuber, *Portrait of Daniel Rose*, 1998. Oil on paper, 85 x 120 (33 3/8 x 47 1/4). Courtesy the artist

45 (below left) Georgina Starr, *Starvision (Danny Rose comic)*, 1997. Drawing. Courtesy the artist

45 (below centre) Oliver Hangl, *Daniel Rose Museum 1*, 1997. Installation view. Courtesy the artist

45 (below right) Oliver Hangl, *Daniel Rose from A–Z*, 1998. Audio CD. Courtesy the artist

46 Ria Pacquée, from the series *Madame going on pilgrimage to Lourdes*, 1989. Colour photograph on canvas, 50 x 70 (19 5/8 x 27 1/2). Courtesy the artist

47 Ria Pacquée, from the series *Madame at carnival in Cologne*, 1989. Colour photograph on canvas, 50 x 70 (19 5/8 x 27 1/2). Courtesy the artist

48 Ria Pacquée, from the series *Madame goes to see the horse racing show*, 1989. Colour photograph on canvas, 50 x 70 (19 5/8 x 27 1/2). Courtesy the artist

49 (above) Ria Pacquée, from the series *Madame visiting the National Garden Festival, hoping to see the Princess*, 1990. Colour photograph on canvas, 50 x 70 (19 5/8 x 27 1/2). Courtesy the artist

49 (centre) Ria Pacquée, from the series *Madame at carnival in Cologne*, 1989. Colour photograph on canvas, 50 x 70 (19 5/8 x 27 1/2). Courtesy the artist

49 (below) Ria Pacquée, from the series *Madame visiting the National Garden Festival, hoping to see the Princess*, 1990. Colour photograph on canvas, 50 x 70 (19 5/8 x 27 1/2). Courtesy the artist

50 Ria Pacquée, from the series *The girl who was never asked to marry*, 1988. Colour photograph on canvas, 50 x 70 (19 5/8 x 27 1/2). Courtesy the artist

52 Andy Warhol, *Camouflage Self-Portrait*, 1986. Silkscreen ink on synthetic polymer paint on canvas, 203.2 x 203.2 (80 x 80). © The Andy Warhol Foundation for the Visual Arts, Inc./ARS, NY and DACS, London 2004

53 (above left) Andy Warhol, *Self-Portrait in Drag (Long Reddish-Brown Wig and Plaid Tie)*, 1981/82. Polaroid photograph, 10.8 x 8.6 (4 1/4 x 3 3/8). © The Andy Warhol Foundation for the Visual Arts, Inc./ARS, NY and DACS, London 2004

53 (above right) Andy Warhol, *Self-Portrait in Drag*, 1981. Polaroid photograph, 10.8 x 8.6 (4 1/4 x 3 3/8). © The Andy Warhol Foundation for the Visual Arts, Inc./ARS, NY and DACS, London 2004

53 (below left) Andy Warhol, *Self-Portrait in Drag (with Black Wig)*, 1981/82. Polaroid photograph, 10.8 x 8.6 (4 1/4 x 3 3/8). © The Andy Warhol Foundation for the Visual Arts, Inc./ARS, NY and DACS, London 2004

53 (below right) Andy Warhol, *Self-Portrait in Drag (with Bouffant Wig)*, 1981/82. Polaroid photograph, 10.8 x 8.6 (4 1/4 x 3 3/8). © The Andy Warhol Foundation for the Visual Arts, Inc./ ARS, NY and DACS, London 2004

55 (above) Andy Warhol, *Self-portrait (in Interview T-Shirt)*, 1977/78. Polaroid photograph, 10.8 x 8.6 (4 1/4 x 3 3/8). © The Andy Warhol Foundation for the Visual Arts, Inc./ARS, NY and DACS, London 2004

55 (below) Andy Warhol, *Self-portrait (back, red T-Shirt)*, 1977/78. Polaroid photograph, 10.8 x 8.6 (4 1/4 x 3 3/8). © The Andy Warhol Foundation for the Visual Arts, Inc./ARS, NY and DACS, London 2004

57 (above) 138 of Andy Warhol's 610 *Time Capsules*, as exhibited/stored in The Andy Warhol Museum, Pittsburgh. © The Andy Warhol Foundation for the Visual Arts, Inc./ ARS, NY and DACS, London 2004. Photo Richard Stoner

57 (below) Contents of Andy Warhol's *Time Capsule 44*, dated mainly 1950–1973. Archives of The Andy Warhol Museum, Pittsburgh. © The Andy Warhol Foundation for the Visual Arts, Inc./ARS, NY and DACS, London 2004. Photo Richard Stoner

58 Jeff Koons, *The New Jeff Koons*, 1980. Duratran, fluorescent light box, 106.7 x 81.3 x 20.3 (42 x 32 x 8). © Jeff Koons. Photo Greg Gorman

59 Jeff Koons, *Art Magazine Ads (Artforum)*, 1988–89. Lithograph, 114 x 94 (44 7/8 x 37). © Jeff Koons. Photo Greg Gorman

60 (left) Jeff Koons, *Art Magazine Ads (Art In America)*, 1988–89. Lithograph, 114 x 94 (44 7/8 x 37). © Jeff Koons. Photo Greg Gorman

60 (right) Jeff Koons, *Art Magazine Ads (Arts)*, 1988–89. Lithograph, 114 x 94 (44 7/8 x 37). © Jeff Koons. Photo Greg Gorman

61 Jeff Koons, *Art Magazine Ads (Flash Art)*, 1988–89. Lithograph, 114 x 94 (44 7/8 x 37). © Jeff Koons. Photo Greg Gorman

62 (left) RASSIM®, *I love Denitsa*, 1996. Colour photograph, 29 x 21 (11 3/8 x 8 1/4). Courtesy the artist. Photo © A. Tsvetanov

62 (right) RASSIM®, *RASSIM®*, 1996. Installation view. Small poster and cartoon images, 29 x 21 (11 3/8 x 8 1/4); 13 x 4.5 (5 1/8 x 1 3/4). Courtesy the artist. Photo © A. Tsvetanov

63 (left) RASSIM®, *Self-portrait with cigarette*, 1995. Video still, from 10-minute video. Courtesy the artist

63 (right) RASSIM®, *Self-portrait with GSM*, 1998. Inkjet print, 120 x 180 (47 1/4 x 70 7/8). Courtesy the artist. Photo © A. Tsvetanov

64 RASSIM®, *Corrections*, 1996–98. Video stills. Courtesy the artist

65 (left) RASSIM®, *Corrections (Before)*, 1996. Inkjet print, 210 x 90 (82 5/8 x 35 3/8). Courtesy the artist. Photo © A. Tsvetanov

65 (right) RASSIM®, *Corrections (After)*, 1998. Inkjet print, 210 x 90 (82 5/8 x 35 3/8). Courtesy the artist. Photo © A. Tsvetanov

66 (above) Cindy Sherman, *Untitled Film Still #4*, 1977. Black and white photograph, 20.3 x 25.4 (8 x 10). Courtesy the artist and Metro Pictures, New York

66 (below) Cindy Sherman, *Untitled Film Still #21*, 1978. Black and white photograph, 20.3 x 25.4 (8 x 10). Courtesy the artist and Metro Pictures, New York

67 Cindy Sherman, *Untitled Film Still #37*, 1978. Black and white photograph, 25.4 x 20.3 (10 x 8). Courtesy the artist and Metro Pictures, New York

68 Christian Boltanski, *Christian Boltanski à 5 ans 3 mois de distance*, 1970. Collage, black and white photographs, dimensions variable. © Christian Boltanski. Courtesy Yvon Lambert, Paris

69 Christian Boltanski, *Reconstitution de chansons qui ont été chantées à Christian Boltanski entre 1944 et 1946*, 1971. Record, 18 x 18 (7 1/8 x 7 1/8). © Christian Boltanski. Courtesy Yvon Lambert, Paris

70 Christian Boltanski, *Saynète comique*, 1974. Black and white photographs, 24 x 30 (9 3/8 x 11 7/8). © Christian Boltanski. Courtesy Yvon Lambert, Paris

74 Mary Kelly, *Post-Partum Document 1973–79, Documentation II, Analysed Utterance and Related Speech Events*, 1975. Mixed media, 20.5 x 25.5 (8 x 10). Courtesy the artist and Collection Art Gallery of Ontario, Toronto

75 Mary Kelly, *Post-Partum Document 1973–79, Documentation II, Analysed Utterance and Related Speech Events*, 1975. Installation view. Courtesy the artist and Collection Art Gallery of Ontario, Toronto

76 Mary Kelly, *Post-Partum Document 1973–79, Documentation III, Analysed Markings and Diary Perspective Schema*, 1975. Mixed media, 35.5 x 20 (14 x 11). Courtesy the artist and Collection Tate Modern, London

77 Mary Kelly, *Post-Partum Document 1973–79, Documentation III, Analysed Markings and Diary Perspective Schema*. Installation view. Courtesy the artist and Collection Tate Modern, London

78 Gerhard Richter, *Atlas: Fotos aus Zeitschriften, Tafel Nr. 73*, 1964. Black and white newspaper photographs, 51.7 x 66.7 (20 3/8 x 26 1/4). Courtesy the artist and Lenbachhaus, Munich

79 Gerhard Richter, *Atlas: Albumfotos, Tafel Nr. 2*, 1962–66. Black and white photographs, 51.7 x 66.7 (20 3/8 x 26 1/4). Courtesy the artist and Lenbachhaus, Munich

80 Gerhard Richter, *Atlas: S. mit Moritz, 1995, Tafel Nr. 605*, 1995. Colour photographs, 51.7 x 66.7 (20 3/8 x 26 1/4). Courtesy the artist and Lenbachhaus, Munich

81 Gerhard Richter, *Atlas: S. mit Moritz, 1995, S. mit Ella, 1996, Tafel Nr. 606*, 1995/96.

Colour photographs, 51.7 x 66.7 (20 3/8 x 26 1/4). Courtesy the artist and Lenbachhaus, Munich

82 Gerhard Richter, *Atlas*, 1998. Installation view. Courtesy the artist and Lenbachhaus, Munich

84 Elke Krystufek, *Collector Krystufek with Ketty La Rocca*, 2002. Colour print, dimensions variable. Courtesy the artist and Kunsthalle Wien, Vienna

85 (above) Elke Krystufek, *Satisfaction*, 1994. Performance. Courtesy the artist. Photo Attilio Maranzano

85 (below left) Elke Krystufek, *Performance for short sighted people*, 2002. Performance. Courtesy the artist and Kenny Schachter conTEMPorary, New York

85 (below right) Elke Krystufek, *I speak painting*, 2002. Performance. Courtesy the artist and Emily Tsingou Gallery, London

86 (left) Elke Krystufek, *Europa arbeitet in Deutschland*, 2001. Acrylic on canvas, 180 x 140 (70 7/8 x 55 1/8). Courtesy GEORG KARGL Fine Arts, Vienna

86 (right) Elke Krystufek, *Your Daddy*, 2001. Acrylic on canvas, 70 x 50 (27 1/2 x 19 5/8), Private collection. Courtesy GEORG KARGL Fine Arts, Vienna

87 Elke Krystufek, *Reminder (Exiter)*, 2001. Acrylic on canvas, 180 x 140 (70 7/8 x 55 1/8). Private collection. Courtesy GEORG KARGL Fine Arts, Vienna

88 (above) Tracey Emin, *Exorcism of the last painting I ever made*, 1996. Installation view. Mixed media. Dimensions of room 390 x 430 (153 1/2 x 169 1/4). © The artist. Courtesy Jay Jopling/White Cube (London). Photo Stephen White

88 (below) Tracey Emin, *My Bed*, 1998. Installation view. Mattress, linens, pillows, rope, various memorabilia, 79 x 211 x 234 (31 x 83 x 92). © The artist. Courtesy Jay Jopling/White Cube (London). Photo Stephen White

89 Tracey Emin, *Everyone I Have Ever Slept With 1963–1995*, 1995. Installation view. Appliquéd tent, mattress and light, 122 x 245 x 215 (48 x 96 1/2 x 84 1/2). © The artist. Courtesy Jay Jopling/White Cube (London). Photo Stephen White

90 Sophie Calle, *Suite vénitienne*, 1980 (detail). Black and white photograph, 17.1 x 23.6 (6 3/4 x 9 1/4). Courtesy the artist and Emmanuel Perrotin. © ADAGP, Paris and DACS, London 2004

91 Sophie Calle, *Suite vénitienne*, 1980 (details). Black and white photographs. Courtesy the artist and Emmanuel Perrotin. © ADAGP, Paris and DACS, London 2004

92 Sophie Calle, *Suite vénitienne*, 1980 (details). Black and white photographs. Courtesy the artist and Emmanuel Perrotin. © ADAGP, Paris and DACS, London 2004

93 Sophie Calle, *The Shadow (La filature)*, 1981 (detail). Installation view. 9 black and white photographs, 1 colour photograph, 11+1 texts, 25.8 x 17.7 (10 1/8 x 6 7/8) and 16.7 x 67.5 (6 5/8 x 26 5/8) (photographs), 71.5 x 245 (28 1/8 x 96 3/8) and 30 x 21.5 (11 7/8 x 8 3/8) (texts), 17.1 x 23.6 (6 3/4 x 9 1/8). Courtesy the artist and Emmanuel Perrotin. © ADAGP, Paris and DACS, London 2004

95 Antje Schiffers, *bin in der steppe*, 2002 (details). Colour photographs, each 13 x 18 (5 x 7). Courtesy the artist

96 Antje Schiffers, *bin in der steppe*, 2002 (details). Colour photographs, each 13 x 18 (5 x 7). Courtesy the artist

97 Antje Schiffers, *bin in der steppe*, 2002. Installation view. Colour photographs, wall drawing, video. Courtesy the artist

98 Christine Hill, *Volksboutique Reference Library*, 2001. Installation view. Courtesy Volksboutique, Galerie EIGEN+ART, Berlin, and Ronald Feldman Fine Arts, New York. Photo Uwe Walter

99 (above left) Christine Hill, *Volksboutique Prototype*, 1995. Installation view. Courtesy

Volksboutique, Galerie EIGEN+ART, Berlin, and Ronald Feldman Fine Arts, New York. Photo Uwe Walter

99 (above right) Christine Hill, *Volksboutique Workspace*, 1996–97. Installation view. Courtesy Volksboutique, Galerie EIGEN+ART, Berlin, and Ronald Feldman Fine Arts, New York. Photo Uwe Walter

99 (below left) Christine Hill, *Tourguide Office*, 1999. Installation view. Courtesy Volksboutique, Galerie EIGEN+ART, Berlin, and Ronald Feldman Fine Arts, New York. Photo Lary Lamay

99 (below right) Christine Hill, *Pilot Production Office*, 2000. Installation view. Courtesy Volksboutique, Galerie EIGEN+ART, Berlin, and Ronald Feldman Fine Arts, New York. Photo Lary Lamay

100 Christine Hill, *Desk.Retro*, 2000. Photo Artslut Archive. Courtesy Volksboutique

102 Jun Yang, *coming home – daily structures of life – version D 00*, 2001. Installation view. Courtesy the artist and Galerie Martin Janda, Vienna

103 Jun Yang, *coming home – daily structures of life – version D 00*, 2000. Video stills, from 20-minute video. Courtesy the artist and Galerie Martin Janda, Vienna

104 Jun Yang, *coming home – daily structures of life – version D 00*, 2000. Video stills, from 20-minute video. Courtesy the artist and Galerie Martin Janda, Vienna

105 Jun Yang, *ARISE! ARISE! ARISE!*, 2001. Landscape model, electric train, model houses, sound installation. Courtesy the artist and Galerie Martin Janda, Vienna. Photo H.-Ch. Schink

106 Jun Yang, *Jun Yang and Soldier Woods*, 2001. Video stills, from 10-minute video. Courtesy the artist and Galerie Martin Janda, Vienna

107 Anny and Sibel Öztürk, *Re-Collection (Frankfurter Zimmer)*, 2000. Installation view. Courtesy the artists

108 Anny and Sibel Öztürk, *Visualize (Dresdner Zimmer)*, 2001. Installation view. Courtesy the artists

109 Anny and Sibel Öztürk, *Preparations for a Journey*, 2002. Installation view. Courtesy the artists

110–11 TOBIAS Z., *Neustädter Nachrichten*, 2001. Mixed media. Courtesy the artists

112 Rirkrit Tiravanija, *Untitled 2002 (Schindler)*, 2002. Installation view: Secession, Vienna. Courtesy the artist and Neugerriemschneider, Berlin

113 Rirkrit Tiravanija, *Untitled 1996 (tomorrow is another day)*, 1996. Installation view: Kölnischer Kunstverein, Cologne. Courtesy the artist and Neugerriemschneider, Berlin

114 Rirkrit Tiravanija, *Untitled 1999 (caravan)*, 1999. Installation view: Fundaciò La Caixa, Barcelona. Courtesy the artist and Neugerriemschneider, Berlin

116–19 Adrian Piper, *A Tale of Avarice and Poverty*, 1985. Black and white photograph and texts. Courtesy the artist and Wadsworth Atheneum, Hartford, Connecticut

120 Shirana Shahbazi, [Shahrzad-04-2002], from *Goftare Nik/Good Words*, 2000–2. Colour photograph. Courtesy the artist and Galerie Bob van Orsouw, Zurich

121 Shirana Shahbazi, [Tehran-11-1998], from *Goftare Nik/Good Words*, 2000–2. Colour photograph. Courtesy the artist and Galerie Bob van Orsouw, Zurich

122 Shirana Shahbazi, [Manzareh-06-2002], from *Goftare Nik/Good Words*, 2000–2. Colour photograph. Courtesy the artist and Galerie Bob van Orsouw, Zurich

123 Shirana Shahbazi, [Mard-03-2000], from *Goftare Nik/Good Words*, 2000–2. Colour photograph. Courtesy the artist and Galerie Bob van Orsouw, Zurich

124 Shirana Shahbazi, [Heyvan-01-2002], from *Goftare Nik/Good Words*, 2000–2. Colour photograph. Courtesy the artist and Galerie Bob van Orsouw, Zurich

125 Shirana Shahbazi, *Goftare Nik/Good Words*, 2001. Installation view: GFZK Leipzig. Courtesy the artist and Galerie Bob van Orsouw, Zurich. Photo H.-Ch. Schink

126–27 William Kentridge, *Johannesburg, Second Greatest City after Paris*, 1989. Charcoal drawings. Courtesy the artist

128 (above) Tracey Rose, *Ciao Bella: Ms Cast Series 'Bunnie'*, 2002. Lambda photographic print, 118.5 x 119 (46 ^{5}/$_8$ x 46 ^{7}/$_8$). Courtesy The Goodman Gallery, Johannesburg, and The Project

128 (below) Tracey Rose, *Ciao Bella: Ms Cast Series 'Venus Baartman'*, 2002. Lambda photographic print, 119 x 119 (46 ^{7}/$_8$ x 46 ^{7}/$_8$). Courtesy The Goodman Gallery, Johannesburg, and The Project

129 (above left) Tracey Rose, *Ciao Bella: Ms Cast Series 'Cicciolina'*, 2001. Lambda photographic print, 117.5 x 118 (46 ^{1}/$_4$ x 46 ^{3}/$_8$). Courtesy The Goodman Gallery, Johannesburg, and The Project

129 (above right) Tracey Rose, *Ciao Bella: Ms Cast Series 'Lovemefuckme'*, 2001. Lambda photographic print, 118 x 118 (46 ^{3}/$_8$ x 46 ^{3}/$_8$). Courtesy The Goodman Gallery, Johannesburg, and The Project

129 (below left) Tracey Rose, *Ciao Bella: Ms Cast Series 'Mami'*, 2001. Lambda photographic print, 117.5 x 119 (46 ^{1}/$_4$ x 46 ^{7}/$_8$). Courtesy The Goodman Gallery, Johannesburg, and The Project

129 (below right) Tracey Rose, *Ciao Bella: Ms Cast Series 'MAQEII'*, 2002. Lambda photographic print, 118.5 x 118.5 (46 ^{5}/$_8$ x 46 ^{5}/$_8$). Courtesy The Goodman Gallery, Johannesburg, and The Project

130 (above left) Tracey Rose, *Ciao Bella: Ms Cast Series 'Lolita'*, 2001. Lambda photographic print, 119 x 119 (46 ^{7}/$_8$ x 46 ^{7}/$_8$). Courtesy The Goodman Gallery, Johannesburg, and The Project

130 (above right) Tracey Rose, *Ciao Bella: Ms Cast Series 'Regina Coeli'*, 2002. Lambda photographic print, 118.5 x 133 (46 ^{5}/$_8$ x 52 ^{3}/$_8$). Courtesy The Goodman Gallery, Johannesburg, and The Project

130 (below left) Tracey Rose, *Ciao Bella: Ms Cast Series 'Silhouetta'*, 2002. Lambda photographic print, 119 x 119 (46 7/8 x 46 7/8). Courtesy The Goodman Gallery, Johannesburg, and The Project

130 (below right) Tracey Rose, *Ciao Bella: Ms Cast Series 'San Pedro'*, 2002. Lambda photographic print, 117.5 x 118 (46 1/4 x 46 3/8). Courtesy The Goodman Gallery, Johannesburg, and The Project

133 Ilya Kabakov, *10 Characters: The Man Who Flew into Space from his Apartment*, 1981–88. Installation view. Mixed media. Courtesy Ilya and Emilia Kabakov. Photo D. James Dee

134 (above left and right) Ilya Kabakov, *10 Characters*, 1988. Installation view. Mixed media. Courtesy Ilya and Emilia Kabakov. Photo D. James Dee

134 (below left) Ilya Kabakov, *10 Characters: The Short Man (The Bookbinder)*, 1988. Installation view. Mixed media. Courtesy Ilya and Emilia Kabakov. Photo D. James Dee

134 (below right) Ilya Kabakov, *10 Characters: The Man Who Never Threw Anything Away*, 1988. Installation view. Mixed media. Courtesy Ilya and Emilia Kabakov. Photo D. James Dee

136 (above left) Ilya Kabakov, *The Boat of My Life*, 1993. Drawing, 21.7 x 28 (8 1/2 x 11). Courtesy Ilya and Emilia Kabakov

136 (above right) Ilya Kabakov, *The Boat of My Life*, 1995. Drawing. Courtesy Ilya and Emilia Kabakov

136 (below left and right) Ilya Kabakov, *The Boat of My Life,* 1993. Installation view. Courtesy Ilya and Emilia Kabakov. Photo Margerita Spiluttini

137 Johannes Wohnseifer, *10-17-71*, 2002. Digital print, 13.6 x 9.7 (5 3/8 x 3 7/8). Courtesy the artist and Galerie Gisela Capitain, Cologne

138–39 Johannes Wohnseifer, *Freeway Race (Autobahnrennen)*, 2001. Production still. Courtesy the artist and Galerie Gisela Capitain, Cologne

140 Johannes Wohnseifer, *Untitled*, 2002. Collage, 23.5 x 17.3 (9 1/4 x 6 7/8). Courtesy the artist and Galerie Gisela Capitain, Cologne

141 Johannes Wohnseifer, *Almost Abstract Study*, 2002. Collage, 26.5 x 20.3 (10 3/8 x 8). Courtesy the artist and Galerie Gisela Capitain, Cologne

142 Johannes Wohnseifer, *09-15-95*, 2002. Collage, 26.8 x 19.1 (10 5/8 x 7 1/2). Courtesy the artist and Galerie Gisela Capitain, Cologne

144 Johanna Kandl, *Fritzelack*, 2002. Tempera on canvas, 290 x 250 (114 1/8 x 98 3/8). Courtesy Galerie Christine König, Vienna. Photo Sammlung Essl (Klaus Vyhnalek)

145 (above) Johanna Kandl, *Visiting Mega-bauMax (Betriebsbesichtigung Mega-bauMax)*, 2002. Tempera on wood, 115 x 150 (45 1/4 x 59). Courtesy Galerie Christine König, Vienna. Photo Sammlung Essl (Klaus Vyhnalek)

145 (below) Johanna Kandl, *Visit to the Studio (Atelierbesuch)*, 2002. Tempera on wood, 60 x 80 (23 5/8 x 31 1/2). Courtesy Galerie Christine König, Vienna. Photo Sammlung Essl (Klaus Vyhnalek)

146 Johanna Kandl, *o.T. (Der Eingang zur Baustelle...)*, 1999. Tempera on wood, 120 x 170 (47 1/4 x 66 7/8). Courtesy Galerie Christine König, Vienna. Photo H. & J. Kandl

147 Johanna Kandl, *o.T. (In Wjasma)*, 1999. Tempera on wood, 60 x 80 (23 5/8 x 31 1/2). Courtesy the artist and Galerie Altnöder, Salzburg. Photo H. & J. Kandl

148 (above) Oliver Musovik, *My Best Friends*, 2002. Inkjet print, 30 x 42 (11 7/8 x 16 5/8). Courtesy the artist

148 (below) Oliver Musovik, *Neighbours*, 1999. Inkjet print, 30 x 42 (11 7/8 x 16 5/8). Courtesy the artist

149–50 Oliver Musovik, *My Best Friends*, 2002. Inkjet prints, 30 x 42 (11 7/8 x 16 5/8). Courtesy the artist

151 Oliver Musovik, *My Best Friends*, 2002. Installation view. Courtesy the artist

152–54 Anri Sala, *Intervista*, 1998. Video stills, from 26-minute video. Courtesy the artist and Galerie Chantal Crousel, Paris

156 Dorit Margreiter, *Short Hills*, 1999–2000. Video still, from 16-minute video. Courtesy Galerie Krobath Wimmer, Vienna

157 Dorit Margreiter, *Short Hills*, 2000. Colour photograph. Courtesy Galerie Krobath Wimmer, Vienna

159 Dorit Margreiter, *Studiocity*, 1998. Video stills, from 12-minute video. Courtesy the artist and Galerie Krobath Wimmer, Vienna

160 Dorit Margreiter, *Short Hills*, 1999–2000. Installation view: Frankfurter Kunstverein, 2000. Courtesy Galerie Krobath Wimmer, Vienna

161 Ruby Sircar, *@mp (asiatic mode of production)*, 2002. Black and white photo print, 21 x 40 (8 1/4 x 15 3/4). Courtesy the artist

162 Ruby Sircar, *@mp (asiatic mode of production)*, 2002. Black and white photo print, 21 x 40 (8 1/4 x 15 3/4). Courtesy the artist

163 (above) Ruby Sircar, *@mp (asiatic mode of production)*, 2002. Black and white photo print, 21 x 40 (8 1/4 x 15 3/4). Courtesy the artist

163 (below) Ruby Sircar, *@mp (asiatic mode of production)*, 2001. Installation view. Courtesy the artist. Photo H.-Ch. Schink

164–65 Rosemarie Trockel, *o.T.*, 1993. Mixed materials in show-case, 59.3 x 160 x 15 (23 3/8 x 63 x 5 7/8). Courtesy Galerie Sprüth/Magers, Cologne. Photo Bernhard Schaub

168 Friedl Kubelka, *1. Jahresporträt 1972–73, 'Spiegel'*, 1972–73 (detail). Black and white photograph. Courtesy Generali Foundation, Vienna

169 Friedl Kubelka, *1. Jahresporträt 1972–73, 'Spiegel'*, 1972–73 (detail). Black and white photograph. Courtesy Generali Foundation, Vienna

171 Moira Zoitl, *Ich war 0.doc*, 2001. Video stills. Courtesy the artist

172 (left and right) Moira Zoitl, *Ich war 0.doc*,
2001. Installation views: Kunstverein Wolfsburg.
Courtesy the artist. Photos Ralf Hoedt

173 Moira Zoitl, *base mix*, 1998. Video stills.
Courtesy the artist

174 Moira Zoitl, *base mix*, 1998. Set photo.
Courtesy the artist. Photo Ralf Hoedt

175 Moira Zoitl, *base mix*, 1998. Video still.
Courtesy the artist

176 Nan Goldin, *Self-portrait on the rocks,
Levanzo, Sicily*, 1999. Colour Cibachrome.
© Nan Goldin. Courtesy the artist

177 (above) Nan Goldin, *Jens' hand on
Clemens' back, Paris*, 2001. Colour Cibachrome.
© Nan Goldin. Courtesy the artist

177 (below) Nan Goldin, *Valerie in the light,
Bruno in the dark, Paris*, 2001. Colour
Cibachrome. © Nan Goldin. Courtesy the artist

178 Nan Goldin, *Cross in the fog, Brides-les-
Bains, France*, 2002. Colour Cibachrome.
© Nan Goldin. Courtesy the artist

179 Nan Goldin, *Fatima candles, Portugal*, 1998.
Colour Cibachrome. © Nan Goldin. Courtesy the
artist

181–82 Wiebke Loeper, from the *Lad* series,
1996–97. Book and photographs, 39 x 53 (15 $^3/_8$
x 20 $^7/_8$). Courtesy J. J. Heckenhauer, Berlin.

INDEX OF ARTISTS

Page numbers in *italics* refer to illustrations